Hildegard:
A Tale of Survival
in Hitler's Germany

God Bless America
Hildegard

Hildegard C. Larsen

Acknowledgements

I would like to express my gratitude to my cherished friends: Dr. Sharon Huddleston, Ph.D. and Dr. Nancy Hamilton, Ph.D. for their hours of formatting that converted my words into a book and for creating the covers for the book; Natalie Meehan for the joy and love she showed me while typing my hand written story; Liz Thorpe for her many hours of editing; Helen Kielty for her continuous comfort and support that I needed so much; Carol Ratchford for her feedback on the manuscript; and, Dr. Robert Neymeyer, Ph.D. for his helpful advice.

This thank you comes from my heart to all my friends who prayed for me throughout the entire writing process.

Part 1

Before World War II

I need to tell my story because World War II is still so deep in my heart. For so many years, even before the war, we lived in fear. Children had to learn the meaning of war in their young years. With me, it started when I was six years old. My innocent and carefree childhood ended, I lost my freedom in many ways.

Losing freedom of speech, religion and even play were our way of life, all ages lived in fear of being separated from their families, and yes, it did happen. So many kids will never feel Mom's and Dad's arms around them, never feel the unconditional love parents can give.

I believe the Lord was the light on our path, throughout our lives. It is that light that has given me the courage to tell my story. I did not want your children or grandchildren ever to go through times like my family and me. Many prayers and a strong push from God helped me find the courage to write our life story.

I never thought I could do that; then it came to mind that I have to educate my heart and mind which only can be the key to a better life, love, compassion and peace.

I have seen the good and the bad that life has to offer. It all started in my childhood. But even the bad taught me good lessons for a great life.

This story is about our family life formed in love, joy, sorrow, and courage in Germany and war-torn Germany. Dawillen, Lituania, a quiet agrarian village, is where my story begins.

I was born on the farm that had been cultivated by three generations of my father's family. I was the first of five children. My brothers were Arno and Horst, and my sisters were Elinor and Ruth. This farm was graced with a beautiful farmhouse, built to last for more than 100 years for generations to come, surrounded by lots of beautiful trees, with a fence around the house and gardens, and a large bell fastened on the pole to ring if you wanted to visit.

My childhood on the farm was short-lived. Political unrest grew and my father, concerned with the safety of his family, left the farm, even though he was the firstborn and expected to take over the family business.

I was two years old when we moved to Germany to a little town, Nonnenberg. My mom gave birth to a little boy, Arno.

Dad could not find the work he would have liked and we moved to East Prussia to a little village near the Steinorter Forest, a very beautiful part of Germany. Lots of large farms and beautiful homes, big woods with lots of animals, the wild ones were fenced in. There were lovely, large lakes.

I remember, I always loved to sit on the window before my bedtime and sing goodnight to all the animals. If I did not have enough songs, I made them up. Dad had to stop me many times, ask me to go to bed, but I always said, "Papa, I need to sing one more song!"

"O.K.—only one."

Saturday mornings were our times with Dad. We went fishing. Mom came later with the little ones and brought food for the rest of the day. We only had a 10-minute walk to the lake.

The weekends always belonged to us kids with Mom and Dad. Dad made a hand wagon. Mom put pillows and blankets inside. That was a safe haven for the little ones.

We got enough fish for a good breakfast. I am sure no toy could replace those Saturdays and Sundays with our Mom and Dad.

We stayed the whole day on the water, swimming, playing ball, taking our nap. Mom and Dad thought up great water games. Our neighbors often spent the afternoon with us—a very wonderful childhood memory.

Sunday, 10:00 a.m. church service. We had to start very early, had 1 ½ - 1 ¾ hour walk, summer and winter. I believe sometimes we were walking and sleeping. We kids were tired. My brother would often say, "Mama, please talk to me later. I am still sleepy."

Dad started singing songs we all knew. Mama joined in and soon the whole family sang our way to church and back.

We had a little barn. Nobody used it, and it did not belong to us, but we got some little chickens and a rooster and that little barn became our chicken house. We had fresh eggs and Mom used one chicken for our Sunday meal.

Mom got the chicken and the ax. I stood away from her on the side. She put the chicken's neck on the wooden block, lifted the ax, and I passed out.

Mom dropped everything, came to wake me up, the chicken walked away. When I came to, I asked Mom, "Where is the chicken?"

Mom said, "Out there enjoying life!"

Dad found good work and later became the mayor of the town and surrounding area. It was a good and happy life—but how fast life can change.

Hitler's power was growing and evil currents of power and oppression were moving through Germany and beyond. My father was not a proponent of the new politics and refused to support Hitler.

Nazi supporters were placed in all public positions. Dad lost his job. Life became very difficult for our family.

Mom and Dad never let us know how much they worried about their children, but we kids often saw sadness in our parents' faces. I often said, "Mama, I am a kid, but I grow up fast and I understand that our lives are not the same as they were. I just want you to know you can talk to me about everything."

Mom just hugged me and said, "I know, my child. Some people are very bad and we have to be careful in whatever we do or wherever we go. Always talk things over with Mom or Dad first.

Soldiers were hurting us children, throwing stones at our windows at night. That scared us kids. After the third night, Mom opened the window and told the soldiers, "You are hurting my children by playing your games, but if you believe you have to disturb our night's rest, I will hurt at least one of you badly." The soldiers were laughing and did not stop. The next night Mom opened the windows. Stones fell into the room. Mom filled a large bucket with boiling water and rolled it down to the soldiers. They screamed and ran away. That was the end of bad nights.

We lost our freedom in so many ways, losing freedom of speech, religion and even play was our way of life.

I experienced this underlying oppression and tyranny when I was 6 years old. I went to school—a one-hour walk one way. I was worried about greeting the teacher. Should I say, "Good morning, Mr. Teacher" or 'Heil Hitler, Mr. Teacher"? I was not really given the opportunity to decide or even talk to my parents about that. The teacher stood at the classroom door. He was a big Nazi supporter and knew my father did not belong to the party.

I said, "Good morning, Mr. Teacher." He called me over to him and cruelly slapped me hard across my face. I was frightened, could not figure out what I had done wrong. I went into the classroom, with a bad headache. The teacher ignored me. That hurt me the most. I did not tell my parents. I really thought I must have done something wrong.

I was scared to go to school the next day. The teacher stood there again. This time I said, "Heil Hitler, Mr. Teacher" instead of "Good Morning."

He smiled and said "Come." He was very friendly. I walked to him again and he hit my face so hard and said, "That will teach you!" I got so sick to my stomach I thought I would pass out. I turned around and started walking home. I do not know how long it took me. I had a hard time walking and rested from time to time. My eye was swollen closed, my whole face was swollen and I had a very bad headache.

I told my parents about what had happened, and Dad said to Mom, "Take care of our girl." He swung on his bike and went to school. He called the teacher to come out and close the door. A little boy came from the bathroom, heard my Dad and hid behind the clothes rack. He witnessed the whole conversation and more.

Dad said to the teacher, "I am here to greet you the way you greeted my little daughter, so you can feel the pain she is feeling now. And that will also be a warning. Do not hurt my children or any other children anymore."

Dad must have told him really good. We had a substitute teacher for eight or ten days. When the teacher returned to the classroom, he ignored me. I did not like it. I wanted to be seen and heard like the other children. I wanted to learn. If he had a question, I raised my hand like the others. He did not even look at me. I needed to go to the bathroom, lifted my hand to ask for permission. He did not ask me what I wanted, did not want to hear me. Like a little worm, I went on my knees and crawled on the floor out of the classroom and returned that way, I was so ashamed and so scared. I was just 6 years old.

I told my parents about the day at school. "It will not happen again," Dad said. "I will be there early in the morning and have a friendly talk with the teacher and will also ask him to tell you he's sorry." I believe Dad wanted to make it easy for me to go to school again.

Dad came early. The teacher invited him in. Dad asked the teacher if he could talk to the children first for a few minutes. He greeted the children, gave me a smile, told the children how proud he was of everyone and how much he missed them. I was so proud of my Dad.

The kids knew my dad. He was the mayor and also wrote stories every week for the Sunday paper, stories about the children and their lives. Dad was well-known in the community and around and I guess the Nazi supporters expected Dad to become a faithful Hitler supporter, but he had no trust or belief in Hitler. He did what he thought was right for all of us. But that did not give us any peace. We knew Dad was right, but that scary feeling walked with us.

Dad knew a war was in the making and he decided to take the family on a long train ride to visit his parents, grandparents, and the kids' great-grandparents. Grandma still lived on the farm where Dad and I were born.

Mom made two nice dresses for the girls and the boys got suits, and then came the day when Papa said, "Pack your suitcases." That meant our backpacks. We left the day after. Everything was so wonderfully planned. We could not wait for the big, fast train to move into the train station and stop for us. I am sure there were other people waiting, but we could not think of anything but the long, beautiful train coming to pick us up. We stood close to Mom and Dad.

The big train rolled in. I could not believe it. We would be in there for a long time. There were seats in groups of four. Mom and Dad sat on one side and held the two year old; the two boys were across from Dad and Mom. The boys shared the window. I had my place across the aisle by the window. To keep our good manners on the train, not run around and/or disturb people, Dad said we had to help the train to stay on the tracks. If the train moved to the right, we had to lean our bodies that way. If it goes to the left to do the same, and we also had to look out for deer, an easy way to keep us busy.

It was hard work and tiring for us kids. A gentleman sat next to me. When I thought the train went to the right, I pushed that nice gentleman almost from his seat. He asked me why I did that, and I told him that Papa said we should help the train. "Good idea!" he said. "I am going to help the train, too. Is that all right with you?" It was OK. My dad talked to the gentleman for a long time.

Memel, the big city! Time to get out and go to another place to wait for the little train! That sure was a happy train.

The little train was very slow, stopping on almost every street. The train whistle never stopped telling the people, "I am coming!" It was so slow one could get out, pick some wildflowers, and run after the train.

It took almost an hour. The whistle was loud. That was a call for us, Dad said. We had to get out and walk for a little while. That was only for five minutes. Then we came to a beautiful old home. A high fence with two iron French doors graced the farm house. A large bell was hanging on a pole. Papa lifted me up and asked me to ring the bell. I did. A beautiful, elderly lady, dressed in a long black dress with a high lace neck, a hanky looking out of the sleeve, came to greet us. She was smiling and so beautiful. Dad said, "That is your Great-grandma." She put her arms around me, then greeted the other children and Mom and Dad. Then Great-grandpa and Grandma came to greet us. It felt like a dream. Everything was so large, so beautiful, so well taken care of.

Two men came and got all our suitcases and walked off. I said, "Papa, the man took our suitcases." Dad said, "That is OK. I'll explain later."

Great-grandma took us to a small house next to their home. It had many rooms. On the table were flowers, fruit, and chocolate. It was a beautiful dream. We felt loved. Mom gave us the choice to lie down for a while. We were tired.

Later we went to the big house. That is how we thought about it. Mom, Dad, Grandma and Great-grandma showed me the room where Dad and I were born. The little cradle that Dad and I had laid in was still standing there. Dad said, "The room is still the same."

I started crying and asked Mom if I was a happy child. The answer came from Dad. "You were our first born, had great-grandparents, Grandma, three aunts and you loved them all. I am sure you knew it was your family. You were a happy child and a good child." The feelings were overwhelming. Mom took me in her arms and said, "Feelings, great memories...almost too much to take."

I cannot remember my excitement when I was two years old. It was not really very exciting for the rest of the family. My Mom told this story so often. My Great-grandma loved to bake bread. It looked like that was all she did besides planning the daily meals and making sure that everything was on time.

One afternoon Great-grandma put flour into a large wooden container which stood on two chairs. She took a large amount of a water mixture, added that into the flour and worked with her hands for a while to mix it up. She then covered the whole container with a large linen cloth. I could not get it out of my head that Great-grandma was playing in all the flour and sticky dough and did not let me play with her. She just let me watch her.

She was done. We walked out of the room. When she was gone, I stopped playing and sneaked into the room, crawled onto the chair and got into the container. I worked very happily in the dough, lost my shoes and socks. It was so much fun. Why did Great-grandma not let me play?

Mom was looking for me and so was Great-grandma. I guess Mom heard my joy. She opened the door and all she could say, "Oh, girl!"

Mom got me out of the dough, cleaned me up and said, "We need to have a serious talk. You hurt Great-grandma and me." Great-grandma got the shoes and socks out, prepared the dough, and it was baked off for the animals. She started again, but the door was locked.

Mom and I sat on the steps outside and we talked. She made me understand that my wrongdoing did hurt my Great-grandma very much. That was my Mama. She never showed her anger, but she was very good at explaining and made me understand how important it is to ask for forgiveness, that I had to go to Great-grandma, tell her that I was very sorry and would never do that again.

I did, and I was really sad about it. Great-grandma loved me, she forgave me. Later, when we were together Great-grandma took me in her arms and the first words she said in German, "You were in my bread dough, I did not forget!" Then she gave me a big hug.

I love my Dad and Mom for teaching us love and respect, compassion, and forgiveness. I thank the Lord that He blessed me with feelings. I did not see my brothers and sisters growing up. When all of us were together again, I thought how the seeds Dad and Mom planted kept growing in all of us, and we are very thankful.

I am still thankful to my Dad and Mom. The visit to our Great-grandparents was so exciting. Memories still live in my heart.

I wrote about that beautiful farmhouse built to last for many generations to come. There was a high fence around the house and garden with an iron gate and the large bell on a pole.

Great-grandpa showed me his horses which were in a large fenced-in pasture, Great-grandpa's joy. There were other pastures with milk cows and, a large grass runout for chickens which was fenced in with a high fence. I was only seven years old, but I saw that most beautiful picture of life all around me and Great-grandpa standing beside me, holding my hand.

As was the tradition, the men worked in the fields and cared for the animals. The women tended the house and gardens.

Great-grandpa looked at everything with great pride. He loved the folks working for him, as I said before, they were his family, too.

I asked Great-grandpa, "What do you love the most?" He put his arm around my shoulder, we started walking. After a while, he said, "Now I know you were listening to every word I said, and here is my answer. I love my family, I love Great-grandma with all my heart, but I love our Lord Jesus the most. He is my life, my teacher. I believe He walks always beside me or in front of me."

The short time walking with my Great-grandpa made a difference in my young life. I really loved my Great-grandparents. It was so easy to love them and heartwarming to know our family is loved.

My Great-grandparent's home was very simple, but tastefully decorated; large rooms, lots of windows. I mostly remember Great-grandpa's sitting room next to his office and to the family dining room. Close to the large picture window in his sitting room were a heavy table and four chairs. The table was decorated with Great-grandpa's bible. In one corner of the room stood a lovely old-time table with a lamp and two comfortable chairs. On one wall was a very long bookcase with shelves and drawers, books in different languages and pewter decorations. On the wall above the bookcase were two oil paintings, Great-grandma and Great-grandpa. There was a door to Great-grandpa's office. I never was in there. The last wall was decorated with only important newspaper and other paper clippings, everything so nice in order. It looked different, but exciting.

After the main meal, Great- grandpa and Dad went to the sitting room, smoked the pipe and talked. I went right along, sat down and tried to read Great-grandpa's Bible. Then I overheard Great-grandpa saying, "That was not really the way, Son. Come, look at this." Great-grandpa showed my Dad the newspaper clipping. It looked like he knew his papered wall well.

I do not remember seeing the living room.

The family dining room had a large dining table, lots of chairs, a long service table with a silver tray, a coffee-sugar-and creamer service on the tray, a china cabinet with lots of dishes and glasses. In one corner of the room was a round table with two large chairs. The only decoration on the dining table was Great-grandpa's Bible. Always before the meal, he read a small part from the Bible and said grace. It was always happy and enjoyable.

Great-grandma planned the food for the noon meal. It was always a very good meal. The men came from the fields at 11:30 a.m. The bell on the gate called everyone. If the men heard it or not, they were always on time. The meal had to be on the table at 12:00 noon. The men and women asked Great-grandpa to say grace and he never missed. It was the same meal for everyone and the table-setting for the workers was the same as for the family. Great-grandpa treated the work personnel like his own family.

I liked the kitchen. Four women were in the kitchen, cooking, canning, and everything necessary, also taking care of the afternoon coffee for the field workers. The women baked cookies for the afternoon. Great-grandpa always got the first ones as soon as they came out of the oven. His horse was waiting for him, also the lady with coffee. Great-grandpa went to the fields where the people worked. He enjoyed the coffee and cookies with his folks.

Once, Great-grandpa took me along. He lifted me on his horse first, then joined me. That was so exciting and very special, my first time on a horse— and with my Great-grandpa.

On the way home, he asked me, "Did you have a good time?"

"Yes, Great-grandpa.   Everyone was so nice to me." I had the feeling Great-grandpa could not enjoy a cookie without knowing that his "second family", as he named them, had their afternoon break, too.

Our Great-grandparents and Grandma were so loving. I heard them praising Mom and Dad for the wonderful kids they raised, and Grandma asked Dad if he still remembered the sad time the family, including Great-grandparents, gave him by pushing another woman into his life. "Remember, you were supposed to marry a young lady we and her parents picked for you. She was lovely and rich."

But your answer was, "I will marry the person I love, not the money."

Then Great-grandpa said he never had to look for a sweet lady to marry. She was chosen for him by his and her parents. The lovely lady was Great-grandma. "Great-grandma and I have a never-ending love for each other and our love is still growing." I was so young, but I could see the love my Great-grandparents still had for each other. How beautiful life can be!

It was a very special vacation with our Great-grandparents, Grandma, and Aunts. We took a lot of joy, unforgettable memories, and love home.

I often wonder what happened to Dad's family. How did the war affect all of them?

Today I am thinking about my great-grandparents belief in the Bible. Their steadfast faith did provide each one of them with strength, trust, and love to live a good and very happy life.

My Grandma and step-Grandpa also lived on the farm. He was a businessman without a business. Four children were born, four girls, and one boy by the first marriage. He died. The boy became my wonderful Dad.

Grandma's second husband asked her to leave the farm with him and move to the city of Memel, where he could find work. She agreed. When Grandma knew she was pregnant, she divorced her husband and no one saw him again.

Grandma must have had a good reason for divorce. She was kind, loving, but did not spend her money on a person who did not want to work. A little boy was born, she named him Herman. Herman became a ship-builder. He also joined the Marines. After the war he married a lovely lady, a very special person.

She died four years later of cancer. Uncle Herman was heartbroken and died two years later.

I was eight years old. Mom had a difficult pregnancy with her fifth child. This event truly ended my childhood. I became the little Mama for a two, three, and five year old.

Watching the children, cooking the meals, taking care of laundry, all by hand, with the old-fashioned washboard, and hanging everything outside on the clothesline became my work.

Since I was not tall enough to reach the line, my five year old brother pushed a footstool wherever I needed to be. I had to clean the floors very well, because the kids played on the floor.

I read and played with the children just as Mama did, helped the kids to bed, prayed with them, gave each one a kiss, and turned the light off, just like Mom did.

The children were good. Every night before I went to bed, I wrote a short letter to Mom, mostly thanking her for being such a good teacher, a loving Mom, and a wonderful friend, saying we all missed her and loved her.

I often had help. A grandma from another family came to watch the children when I was cooking. Papa needed his meal when he came home from work.

Dad did not spend much time with us kids, but I knew and told the children that Papa had to be with Mama to give her all the love and strength to get well again.

Dad worked all day long. In the morning, he biked first to see Mom, which took almost an hour. Then he went from there to work, and after work to the hospital again. Mostly, he was home at midnight. That was a gift of love Dad gave to Mom, and both passed that gift on to their children.

One night Dad came home late from the hospital. I turned the light on because I wanted to hear about Mom and the unborn baby. Dad came to my room, sat on my bed, took me in his arms and said, " I wish I could make you happy. Our Mama is so ill, and the doctor believes the Lord will take her home."

I shook my head. I did not believe the Lord would take a Mom away from her five children. I said, "No, no, Papa." Dad held me so tight, his tears rolled down my cheeks.

Then I said, "Do not worry, Papa. I will talk to the Lord tomorrow. I know He will listen to me. I will start early in the morning. Then our Lord Jesus will not be so tired." Good thought—I was a child. I just needed to help Papa. He was so unhappy, so lost.

The next morning I asked the children to come to Mom's bed. "We have to pray. We have to ask the Lord to make our Mom well, and let her and the baby come home to us again." The kids understood our prayers. Everyone had tears rolling down their cheeks. My love for my brothers and sister grew like little flowers in my heart. They were such wonderful children.

The thought that my Mom could die made me mentally ill. I was too young to know what really happened to me. The walls in every room started moving, closing me in. They came so close I thought they were going to kill me.

Each time that happened, I had to run out into the woods or fields until that scary feeling was gone. I know I was very ill, but I did not tell my Dad, I did not want to put more worry on him. In the afternoon before we had our evening meal, I played with the children, I tried to be happy, but when I looked at the kids, that scared me. Very sad feelings touched my heart, but I had to be strong.

After about 14 days, Dad came home early, was smiling, and said, "Mama is thanking all of you for your prayers and the love you send daily. Mom will come home soon and bring a beautiful baby girl with her."

I looked at my Dad and said, "You see, Papa, God is good," and I started crying.

Dad took me in his arms and said, "Yes, my daughter, God is good." Then I went to my bedroom, got on my knees and asked the Lord to put the walls back where they belonged and keep them there—and I would not have to be afraid anymore. The Lord heard my prayer. It never happened again. I was so thankful.

Here I am, thinking about my Mom, about the strong belief and trust she had in our Lord, the love she gave day and night to her family. Yes, I love my Mom and Dad dearly, even now.

The stress and fear disappeared, and I never told my parents about the big trouble I was having. I thank you, dear Lord Jesus, for letting me believe in you.

Not far from where we lived was a large, beautiful farm. The owner was a big Nazi supporter. Their apple orchard ran along our driveway from the main street to our home. Lots of branches hung over the fence. One night, as so many before, lots of wind sent some apples over the fence. My brother, 5 years old, and I, ran out to get the apples. We had just picked them up, about eight or nine. We heard somebody calling our names. It was the farm owner's wife. She asked us to come to her and said, very friendly, "I want to show you something. Come with me." She went to the pigs yard with us, took the apples from us, threw them to the pigs and said, "That is where they belong. Now go home." How can that person live with so much hate in her heart? We were just little kids and thankful for a little apple.

We took each other's hands and left. We could not talk. We felt like crying. Close to home my brother stopped and said, "She made a mistake. She made a big mistake. She should not have done that." Then he said, "I know a long way around to the pig yard. Take a big bag. We are going to get us lots of apples." So we did.

Coming home, we told Mom what happened. Mom said, "You are my kids, you sure are my kids!" We were scared, but Mom always made us feel good.

If my parents would have been Nazi supporters, we would not have had to pick up apples from the pig yard. The farm owner would have brought us all the apples, and more, but instead, they hurt us, if possible, everywhere they could.

There was another happening. The farmers asked Mama if she would allow me to wash the milk cans when they returned after delivering the milk. My pay would be three liters of fresh milk daily. Mom said,

"If my daughter would like to do that, it's fine with me. But I will not allow her to lift the heavy cans to their boards to dry."

The farm woman said, "That is OK."

I started working. I knew I did a good job. The owner came to check often, and so did Mom. I washed about ten or twelve cans. When I was almost done, the owner came and said, "Pick the cans up and put them where they belong."

I said, "I am sorry. I cannot lift the heavy cans."

She screamed, "Do it!"

I did not know what to say. She took a good-sized stick, cornered me and hit me many times over my back. I dropped everything and ran home. I was hurting, and Mom found five swollen lines on my back. Mom put an ice pack on it and said, "That woman will be very sorry."

In the evening, after the milking was done, Mom watched the farm woman going to the barn and followed her with a good-sized stick. She went right up to the owner and said, "You will never hurt my children again," and gave her the hurt she gave me and more. Mom went in the evening and got the three liters of milk, and unbelievably, the housekeeper brought three liters of milk after the milking every evening. It must have been guilt.

Two days later the Police stopped at our home. Mom saw the car driving up. She went to the stairs. One of them said, "We have to talk. You hurt the farm owner's wife badly."

The Police officer wanted to take a step up and Mom said to the Police, "You do not have to come upstairs. You told me why you are here and here is my answer. She shall be thankful she did not get more, but she got what she deserved." That was the end of the conversation. My mom is a dear heart of a person, but do not hurt her children.

Before my Dad had to join the military, he asked Mom if she would like to visit her childhood girlfriend. She had not seen her for a long time. Mom was happy. For one day, Mom's place became Dad's responsibility. The next day we walked with mom to the train station, and on the way back home we planned our day. It was nice to be with Papa for one day because during weekdays he had to work. That did not give us much time to enjoy Dad.

We cleaned the home a little, then found a nice place outside near the woods to fix our meals. We just decided to live outside the whole day. We took our naps, said our prayers, and had Papa.

We went early to the train station with Mom. She had a good 30-minute walk from the station to her friend's home. As she started to cross the long bridge, she saw something hanging on the end of the bridge. Walking closer, she saw it was a woman. It was Mom's girlfriend….a beautiful, loving person, a school teacher, a long-time friend to our family. She was a Jewish lady. Mom was scared and ran back to the train station. Mom came home. She was crying bitterly. Dad took Mom in his arms to take a little hurt away, and he said, "That is only the beginning. Maybe she was saved from all the painful things that can happen to the Jews." How right Dad was.

I am thinking of a gruesome experience of my third school year. About fifteen minutes' walk from our school was a little hill with beautiful trees and wild flowers. Once a week we had one hour off school to go there, learn and sing Hitler songs with our music teacher. My Dad always said that I have to be a part of any school activities, and I loved it.

We were sitting on our little mountain and almost at the end of the hour when one of the kids pointed to a tree. Everyone started running and crying. When I looked at that point, I wanted to run, too, but could not. My whole body froze. A soldier was hanging there. I do not know how I got off that little hill, but as long as I went to school, we never visited our little hill again. It must have been the end of school time.

Everyone went home. Since I was not home in time, Dad came to look for me. I was on the way home when I saw Dad on the bike. When I told him, he asked me to go home, that he would check it out. All he said when he returned was, "I am sure you kids must have been so scared."

My Dad was right by saying that he believed Mom's girlfriend, Fanny, was probably saved from all the heartache the Jewish people had to go through before their gruesome death.

We witnessed two families, parents and children, being taken from their homes into a truck by armed soldiers. The family carried along suitcases and boxes. The people were crying. I asked Mom if she knew where they are taking the people and why. Mom waited with her answer a little while, then said, "I really cannot give you an answer, my child. I am sure it was not good."

Dear friends of ours came to our home for a visit. They brought their kids. That made us kids happy...we did not have to go to bed that early. I remember the man talking about getting wood to store for the winter. We only used wood or coal for the kitchen stove and also for the oven to warm the rest of the home. Mom was knitting warm socks for us and the women were talking.

It must have been after midnight when I woke up and noticed lights in our friends' home. I told my Mom in the morning. The next morning the kids did not come. We always walked to school together.

Dad and Mom knew that they were taken. The house was locked. They had six milk cows that needed to be milked, and pigs. But they were gone next day. A horrible life started for the Jews—but what did we know about the torture that was waiting for them?

Knowing a war was coming hurt all of us in a different way. Grandma took our coats and jackets with her, opened the seams, and cleaned everything. She made wider seams and stuffed them with very dry bread pieces she had saved. There were lots of times when we thanked Grandma (Mom's mother) for a handful of bread crumbs.

I have to tell you a little story about my Grandparents (Mom's parents). The Czar, Catherine the Great from Russia, called on people to come to Russia to farm. Grandpa and his long-time love for farming, and Grandma, a young trusting wife, followed the call with hope, praying for a better life. Grandpa was born in Russia and lived there until he was fifteen years old. The two young folks, Grandma and Grandpa, packed up and left for Russia once more. What they found was by far not what Catherine the Great promised. The land was bad, and so were the living quarters. Grandma said she was so disappointed. I am sure Grandpa was, too. He only said, "We are going to make it right, not give up." There was one milk cow and they got some money for a small start.

It was a bad start, but Grandpa did not give up. He gave his labor for, I believe, fourteen years. There was no school, Grandpa was the teacher. The hospital, doctors and stores were almost one-half of a day's travel by cow and wagon. Grandpa was a very religious man. I am sure Grandma was, too, because until she died, you could always find Grandma with the Bible beside her. Grandpa looked at a little hill not far from their farm. Grandma told me that Grandpa sat on this little hill for a long time. He returned home and told Grandma that this hill will be their church. That little hill was the closest to God. Nine children were born, eight boys and one girl. He took each newborn to their church for christening and to ask the Lord to bless and love this little baby. Grandpa took all of his happiness and troubles to the Lord.

Then a bad illness came over the land, typhus. Thousands of people died and the disease reached my

Grandparents' home. Six children died in a period of almost two months. Grandpa made a little cemetery on his land, not far from the home. He built a little casket. Each one got their pillow and was covered with their little blanket and Grandpa lowered his sons into their graves. Grandpa made a cross for each one. Grandma said each time he lowered one of their sons into the grave, Grandpa cried out, "Why, dear Lord, why?"

After they lost six children, Grandpa and Grandma decided to pack up and leave. The Grandparents went to the little hill. They told the Lord that they must leave because they needed to save the three children and Grandpa asked the Lord to bless and guide the family. A very hard time started for the family. There was hurt and sadness in their hearts, but they were very thankful for the three lives saved.

The cow pulled the wagon with bedding, clothes and food. They kept walking towards Lituania. It took the family six months to reach Lituania. Grandma said the hardest, most heartbreaking part was to leave the graves with her six children, but she was thankful for her three children, my mom and two uncles. One of her sons became an auto mechanic master. The youngest son (my Uncle Eduard) became a special violin maker, and he played the violin so wonderfully. However, Uncle Eduard was wounded in World War II, and died.

Mom's desire to learn was great. She became a very good seamstress and was able to make clothing for women and men. At age seventeen, she was hired by a very wealthy family to do all their sewing. She had a very beautiful room, and she was happy about that because that was her first room she could name her own, and also her first good job. She felt welcome and also had a place on the table which was an honor. Before each meal, Great-grandpa read a little from the Bible and said grace before the meal was served. It was a very large house, each child had their own living quarters. The kitchen and dining room were shared, the cooking and cleaning were done by paid personnel.

They had two sons and three daughters. One of their sons and Mom got to know each other and fell in love. He became my Dad.

Grandma was almost 100 years old, never needed a doctor, no glasses, never drove a car or rode in a bus. Once I asked her to come to a movie with me. "What do they do?" she asked. After a long explanation, she agreed to go with me. It was after the war. We were sitting there very comfortably. Grandma had never been in such a big place with comfortable chairs and so many people. Suddenly on the screen a big plane came flying towards the people in the audience. Everyone was so quiet, but not Grandma. She took my hand, pulled me up, and in a loud voice said, "We made it through the war and I am not going to let them kill us now." We walked out. People started clapping. I am sure lots of people knew my Oma.

When Grandma felt it was time to go home to the Lord, she asked the family to call me to come home, if possible. I lived in America with my husband. I loved my Grandma. I still see her shiny eyes and happy face when I walked into her room. We had a wonderful but short conversation. Then Grandma said, "I have to go now. Grandpa is here. He is standing on the foot end of the bed."

"Grandma," I said, and without waiting for what I wanted to say, she said, "You cannot see him." Her last words were, "I am so happy to go. Now I will see my six children I never stopped loving." Everyone in the room kissed her. She asked to be left alone with Grandpa. We left, and Grandma died in peace.

Grandma was a good seamstress. She made all her dresses by hand without a sewing machine. It looked like her hands were a sewing machine—wonderful work, gifted hands. I loved my Grandma, that beautiful, good-hearted lady. Grandma died twenty-nine days before her one-hundredth birthday, and was buried on her daughter's (my Mom's) birthday.

As long as I am with my Grandma and Grandpa, I must tell you a story about my Grandpa and me. We visited Grandpa and Grandma often. We had to run one hour from our home to Oma and Opa. We were used to running everywhere.

My two brothers and I decided to go to Grandpa for some strawberries. He was so proud of his fenced-in strawberry garden. He asked the boys if they would like to go and pick or eat some strawberries. "Yes," the boys said, and I went with them. He opened the gate and let the boys in. I waited to follow, but he said, "Only the boys."

My brother heard that and said, "Do not worry. I will bring you the best strawberries, all you want."

I walked to the house, so very sad, so unhappy. Grandma said, "You look so sad."

I started crying and said, "Grandpa does not love me anymore, Grandma. He hurt me. I was not allowed to get into the strawberry garden, only the boys."

Grandma asked me to sit by her. She said, "Grandpa loves you. I know that, and I do not believe Grandpa wanted to hurt you."

But I was hurt, and my childish thinking was searching for revenge. Grandpa had lots of tomatoes which he shared with my Mom. The living room had a very large window with a nice window sill. Grandpa brought tomatoes in and lined them up on the window sill for Grandma to use and give to other folks.

I stood a long time in front of the tomatoes. There must have been twenty-five or thirty of them. I bit from each tomato a good bite and placed each piece next to the wounded tomato. Then I sat down in the living room waiting for Grandpa. Grandpa had a beautiful, well-trimmed white beard, a handsome Grandpa.

Here came Grandpa, sat in his special chair, took his long pipe and just held it in his mouth. When Grandpa spotted the tomatoes, first he looked at me for a while, then said, "Did you do that?"

"Yes, Grandpa."

"I would like to know why," he asked.

I started crying and asked, "Grandpa, don't you love me anymore? You hurt me so much. You let the boys into the strawberry garden, but would not let me come in. I had to hurt you, too, Grandpa. But now I am sorry."

Grandpa put his pipe back on the little table, held his arms wide open and said, "Come to me." I did. I saw tears in his eyes when he said, "I do love you more than my life and I am deeply sorry I hurt you."

Our Opa and Oma were so special to all of us, loving, understanding, and always ready to listen.

When I told Mom that I hurt Grandpa and what I had done, Mom said, "I know Grandpa loves his grandchildren very much, but I believe it could have been he felt he was walking with his kids who died. We always have to be forgiving."

"We forgave each other, Mama."

A long time before the war started, soldiers on the truck drove to our house asking for Dad. We were playing outside. As Dad came down, two soldiers with guns faced Dad and said, "We are giving you a few minutes to pack some things you need. You have to go with us to be trained in case of war."

Dad said, "I believe you are mistaken. The first call is for men without children, then one and so on. I have five children."

One of the German soldiers pulled the gun and pointed it at Dad and two of them pushed Dad to the wall and said, "If you do not go with us, your family will see something they will never forget the rest of their lives." They would have killed Dad in front of Mom and us kids.

Mom said, "Go, Papa, we will be fine. You will return to us. I know you will always find us." Everyone was crying, hurting. I watched my brothers and sisters, their little arms reaching out to Dad for a hug and kiss. I thought my heart was breaking in pieces. It would not have happened if Dad would have become a Nazi supporter.

I was hurting so much, looking at my Mom, tears rolling down her cheeks. She must have been hurting and so scared to let Papa go so fast without warning. He had to leave five children. What a hateful and sad little world we lived in.

I put my arms around Mom and could only say, "Mama, I will help you with whatever I can. Papa will return to us."

Our daily life became a nightmare. Before long, the market was empty. No fruits, no vegetables—just empty. The black market was blooming, but not many people were able to buy the expensive food. After a few days, the market started working again. We got food stamps for half a loaf of bread, which made two slices per person per day, lard, and one pound of ground beef for the six of us for a week. We could buy some other products to make a meal, but the money would not go that far.

I remember that my four- year-old brother came to Mom and said, "Mama, I am so hungry." Mom asked me to go to the kitchen. "There is a slice of bread. Give it to him."

He took the bread and ran outside. Shortly after, we heard him crying. I went to see what happened and found my brother sitting on the house holding the bread in his little hand, and he said, "I cannot eat that bread." He ran to mama and said, "Mama, this is your bread. You must be hungry. Eat a little."

Mom took that little boy in her arms and said, "I never loved you more, my son." So much love and caring from a four-year-old boy!

Every Sunday we went to church—but without Papa, it was mostly a quiet walk. Mom's tears rolled down her face. I took her hand and both of us were crying. The church inside was different. The altar was not decorated as always. There was only one book on the right side. That was Hitler's "Mein Kampf", and on the left side of the altar, the sword. On the day of the foundation, the day Hitler took control, the Christian cross was removed from all churches.

There was book-burning by Nazis from German and Jewish writers and lots of foreign writers were included. Music from Bach and Beethoven, Mozart and Brahms, I believe were saved. But Mendelssohn was banned. He was a Jew. They weeded all the Jews out of the Great Symphony Orchestra and operas.

It was heartbreaking for everyone, but mostly for the Jewish people. Even today, so many years after the war, I still feel the hurt in my heart for all the people who had to give their lives.

On a sunny day, I played with my brothers and sisters outside. A jeep drove up, and soldiers jumped out, grabbed me and pulled me into the jeep. I begged them to let me go home. I cried, told them that Mom would be so unhappy not knowing where they were taking me. They did not even listen. They took their sandwiches out and ate. I begged for a little bit of sandwich. We had not had our noon meal yet. They did not care.

The soldiers took me to some place underground where they made ammunition. I was cold and scared and hungry. The soldiers picked me up in the evening, took me to a barracks room. There was some food and an old warm-up suit. The door got locked and they left. They must not have had a heart.

I was so scared, so homesick. I cried myself to sleep. I was just a 13 year old kid.

The pickup was 6:00 in the morning to work underground. That went for eight days. I lost a lot of weight, felt ill. Then the same soldiers took me to a hospital, a mental health unit. The doors were locked. I had eight wonderful days, a warm bed, good food, a wonderful, kind doctor and nurses. The day came again when I had to leave the hospital. The doctor told me to be strong and that I would find my way home again. The same people picked me up. The doctor and nurse came to talk to me before they let them take me and told me that I was in the mental health unit at the hospital.

"Do not worry," the doctor said, "everything will be fine again. Believe in yourself and in your Lord Jesus." I made that my goal.

From there, the soldiers took me to a good-sized farm, again a great Nazi-supporter family. They were not good to me. I had to work from 6:00 a.m. to 7:00 p.m. outside, including milking, cleaning the pig stalls and so on. Once a week was cleaning day. I had to clean the whole home, cook the evening meal. Six o'clock p.m., the meal had to be on the table and afterwards I had to clean up the kitchen. I was always so tired.

I loved cleaning, mostly the bedrooms. I took my cleaning rag, crawled under the bed and took a nap. When I heard someone coming, I moved my arms with the damp rag. The owner got me once, asked what I was doing. I said, "Cleaning under the bed where there was a lot of dust."

She only said, "Das ist gut." (That is good.) That was the first praise I got from her. First I felt a little guilty because I did not do what I said I was doing, but I was so tired.

The farmer's son lived with his Grandma. He did not visit his parents often. I believe he was seventeen years old. He came to the pig stalls, watched me working and said, "What are you doing? You are just a kid. Why are you here?"

I told him, and also said, "I want to go home. My Mom does not know where I am." I trusted him, and said, "I did something bad. Your parents did not pay me for my work, but whenever I could, I took a mark, and now I have about ten marks." I said, "I know that was wrong, but I believe the Lord will forgive me for that."

The young man was quiet for a moment, then said, "That's OK". I will go to my Grandma and ask her for the money you need for a train ticket." He came back the next day with the train ticket.

The next night, the window was the only escape, and we ran to the train station. Was I ever thankful to the young man and his Grandma! Two hours later, I left the train, but had a one-hour walk to our home. I was scared, so scared, walking along the woods. Then I heard steps behind me. I thought somebody must have heard that I ran away and I started running for my life.

I heard somebody calling my name, and not only once. Close to our home, I screamed, "Mama, Mama! Open the door!"

Mom heard me and turned the light on. Some windows were open. As we were in the living room, we heard little stones falling on the window. "Oh, no," Mom said, "Not again!"

She opened the window and a voice said, "Don't do anything wrong, Mama. This is Papa."

Was that ever a wonderful, beautiful, loving surprise! We were together again! Lots of hugs and kisses, lots of happy tears. We missed our Dad so much, we needed him. He had a 14 day vacation from the military before the soldiers would be shipped to the fighting fronts, like Poland, or even Russia.

Now comes the best part. My Dad looked at me and said, "Now, I would like to know what you were doing so late at night on the street?" Today I know what he was thinking. I told Papa the whole story. He was sad that I had to go through all that in my young life. Then he said, "There's got to be a little more. How did the train ticket fall into your hands? You did not have money."

"Papa, I thought the Lord would forgive me if I now and then let a mark fall into my pocket. I took from the family. I felt so lonely. I had to work hard and many hours. Then their son, who lived with his grandma, offered his help by asking his grandma for the money. She was happy to help, and I was thankful."

Dad was quiet for a moment, then he said, "Mom and I always taught our children not to steal! "Du solst nicht stehlen!"

"I did not forget, Papa."

"My daughter, you have to tell them why you did that and let them know you are sorry."

"I cannot do that, Papa! I am not sorry. The owners were not good to me. I wanted to go home just to feel Mom's arms around me. I am sure Mom was sad, like I was."

Dad said, "I do understand, and I thank the Lord that you are here with us. But dear child, I want you to go through life without any guilt feelings. I know my children and I know the day will come when you remember, when you will say, 'Thank you, Dad and Mom.' Tomorrow Mom and I will go with you to the train station and a day after, we will visit the family and see what we will decide."

That was the first time in my young life that I had to say, "Sorry for taking money from you. It did not make me feel good and will never happen again." I returned the money and asked for forgiveness.

The lady of the house said, "Are you really sorry?"

"I should not have done it", I said, "but I am thankful I could go home. My parents will be here to visit with you tomorrow." I asked if I could sleep one more night in my bed. No answer. I did my work as always, cleaned the kitchen and went to bed. In the morning I got up, made the breakfast as always and did a little work in the kitchen. I asked how I could reach their son. I did not tell them about the help I got from their son and Grandma. My parents came the next day. There was a friendly conversation.

The lady asked me if I would go and set the table for all of us in the dining room, make coffee, and put the cake she baked on the table. That was the first time she was nice to me.

We were still sitting around the table when my Mom said, "The Missus asked us if we would let you stay here for as long as you want. Mr. and Mrs. promised to make it right for you and also will pay you for your work, which was always very good, they said. Mom told the folks, "It is your decision." I thought for a minute. It would be good. I could help Mama with the money I got, so I decided I would stay, but I wanted to stay with my family as long as Dad was home. That was all right with them.

When I returned to the farm family, life became wonderful. I felt appreciated. I even felt loved. Their son moved back home. He said so often, "I am thankful. You taught my parents love that was missing in our home." Life became wonderful, joyful and caring. I finally got to know the grandma, a lovely lady, and I had the chance to thank her and give her a big hug.

I often had the wish not to be a farm hand. I wanted to find a place to learn something that would improve my life. Six months later I left the farm. I needed to go home. I got a little scared, too. We heard cannon thunder, more so at night. The family understood. They gave me a lot of smoked meat for my family and paid me well. I was sad. The family was sad, too. We found love for each other. I felt like a daughter in their home.

Part 2

During World War 2

I was happy to be home again. I found a school teaching typewriting and shorthand, a three-month course. I heard that a company not far from where we lived was looking for a private secretary. I was excited, I wanted the job. I told Mom about it and Mom smilingly said, "My daughter, you did not learn enough. No experience. They are asking for an experienced person."

"Mama, I learn fast. I can do that."

Mom said only, "You know I wish you all the best, always, but I do not want you to come home unhappy. They are looking for an experienced person."

"OK, Mom." I put my best dress on. It was a dark blue. I curled my hair a little on the ends, put Mama's shoes on—not the high heels—they did not fit, and had about a two-inch heel. My feet hurt so much. I got there about 10:00 a.m. A beautifully dressed lady asked me if she could help me.

"Yes," I said. "I need to talk to the gentleman who is looking for a private secretary."

She said, "He is not here. He comes in late in the afternoon."

"I'll wait."

Her next question: "Do you want to be a private secretary?"

"Yes," I said.

"You are just a kid!"

"I am not! I had to give up being a kid when I was six years old. I will wait here. I have time."

At noon, that lady started un-wrapping her sandwiches and I was so hungry. How could she not know that I was crying for only one-half of the sandwich?

"That is OK," I thought. "Soon I will bring my own sandwiches." I believed that I would win. I needed the job.

It did not take too long, and an elderly gentleman came out of a room beside her. I got up so fast, walked toward him and said, "Are you looking for a private secretary?"

He smiled a little and said, "Yes."

"I would love to have the job. I need the job."

He turned to the secretary and said, "I will have my meal later. I need to talk to this lady first. Hmm. "Lady" he had said. That minute I grew one inch.

The gentleman had a beautiful office and he was very, very friendly. He asked me why I felt this job would be for me.

My answer: "I learned typewriting and shorthand. I am a fast learner, but most of all, my Mom has five children. I am the oldest, and I need to help my Mom to take care of all of us."

He said, "Here is a blank paper and a pencil. Let's do a little shorthand." He had a lot of machines and a few telephones on his desk. He pushed here and there a button and talked. I had the feeling he wasn't talking to me, so I did not write. After a while he said, "Would you read that back to me, please?"

I said, "I did not think you were talking to me. You played with your machines, but we can try again."

He just looked at me for a little while, got up from his chair, came to me, put one hand on my shoulder and said, "I have five children, all girls. I am proud of every one, but I only wish one would be like you."

"Yes," he said. "I'll hire you. I will give you a good secretary. She will teach you and you will become a good secretary."

"Are you going to pay me, too?" I asked.

The gentleman said, "I will pay you very well."

Was I ever thankful, so thankful! Before I could go home and bring the great news to Mom, I had to fill out some papers. That was easy. Then the lady asked how much time I needed to come to work daily. I told her about forty-five minutes, and she said, "A car will pick you up and take you back home."

That minute I was standing on a beautiful white cloud. I had no words, just "thank you."

A wonderful life started. I could help Mom. The worry how to feed the family was gone. I named the gentleman my "Boss". He also got in touch with my Mom.

I loved my work and learned with joy. We had eight wonderful months, but we also knew that it would end soon. We heard the sounds of war coming closer and we started wondering how long we were going to have a home.

Troops were everywhere, walking quickly and some singing Hitler songs. Mom and I were watching, hoping to see Papa. Folks were standing with their hands in prayer, some crying, others very angry. Mom took my hand and we walked away. Mom said, "Our little world is falling apart."

First Poland, then Russia. Wounded soldiers started to return to Germany. What happened to Lituania? We never had a sign of life from our family.

It did not take too long. Loudspeaker trucks drove through the streets asking the people to take what they could and leave town, as we understood there was a possibility of a bomb attack. We only had, I believe, thirty minutes.

Everyone took their backpack, coat, pillow, and blanket. Mom made some cotton bags for each one of us, plastic-lined inside, and put food in each bag in case of emergency. She was a good Mom. She was thinking of everything, even knowing that this would be the final move to nowhere.

We left the home. Everyone looked back one more time before the door closed. I felt the hurt mostly for Mom. She had a big responsibility, five children, Grandma and Grandpa. We picked up on the road and walked again. Homeless.

We looked back a few times. I believe all of us felt like crying loud out. Thinking about it today, it still fills my heart with sadness.

We hung our heads down and walked. We held hands, hoping to give each other strength, but we cried and did not want Mom to see our tears! She knew.

After a while Mom stopped walking, put her arms around us and said, "I am crying with you, my children. I know we will have a hard road to travel. It will take years, but some day, if God wills, we will be very happy again. We will have a home again. Papa will find us. Let's make that our dream, and believe."

A precious gift was given from my great-grandparents, Dad's family, to my Mom and Dad on their wedding day, two beautiful oil portraits about 20 x 22 inches in size. I loved my handsome Dad and Mom in the picture with her wavy dark brown hair and shiny deep brown eyes. All I ever wanted from my parents were the two portraits. The day we became homeless, the day they made us leave everything and walk out of our warm nest, our home, where we were so happy, we took one last look. That was the first time I felt two pairs of sad eyes looking out of those pictures at me. I thought my heart was breaking in pieces. We had to walk away from everything we loved.

We walked. Later that afternoon Mom said, "Let's take a little rest before we go on to find a place for the night to stay." My Mom took me away from the children, tears rolling down her cheeks, and she said, "My daughter, I was thinking for a long time. What would be the best for you, walking together, or going back to the company?"

I wondered why Mom walked this road, but then we always loved to walk along the woods. "I am very sure," she said, "we cannot outrun the Russians. The machine gun and cannon fire are very close. If they get you, you will be hurt, even hurt for the rest of your life. Trust me."

Mom said, "I was fourteen years old when the war (1914 – 1918) started. I hate sending you away. I love you dearly my daughter, my first-born, but I want you to stay alive."

"What do you want me to do, Mama?" I asked.

"It is going to be very hard for all of us to part, but I believe with all my heart it would be better to go back to your workplace. They will always know when to move on, and you will be as safe as possible with them. You can walk through the woods from here. It will take you about three hours."

I knew the woods.

That was the last night we were together. A farmer let us stay in a barn and we made our beds in the straw. The kids fell asleep very fast. Mom and I talked for a long time. Mom said, "Do not worry. I will find you wherever you are. I will hear when you call my name."

It was so hard to leave our home, but very, very sad to walk away from my family, knowing years would part us. I wanted to turn around and run back to Mom and the kids, but I knew it was just as hard for

Mom and for my brothers and sisters. I loved all of them so very much. I knew we would be together again. I also knew that is just a little drop of hope, but I believed and knew Mom would find me.

The company started packing the night our town was bombed. Months later we were sure the bombing was not meant for our town. We believed it was meant for the buildings in the woods. We also believed the buildings were Hitler's offices, because too many soldiers with guns walked around the buildings and woods night and day.

Our first stop was Konigsberg. It was not safe there, and we moved on to Berlin. We slept a few hours and were on the way out of Berlin, because the sirens went off and the company moved on.

The company went to a little town on the Neckar River to build their offices. The women got a ten-day paid vacation, so we were on our own.

The city of Duren was our first stop, a beautiful town. We moved into a hotel, decided to go downtown to find a restaurant. Sirens went off. We followed people to a bunker. The bombs fell, the earth was shaking. I thought it would never end. People were crying, worried about their families, saying, "We will never get out of here." In the bunker, I had the feeling someone was holding me.

The bombing stopped, the fear was gone, and the next problem started.

How do we get out of here? There was equipment, as in every bunker, to use. I hoped it would help us to get out. We had two doors. We worked hard, the bunker filled up with bad, dusty air. Everyone got out safe. The air outside looked like there was a black blanket over us.

There was hardly a house standing, only ruins, stones, gravel, and here and there a small fire. In some places stood a wall, the remains of a home. People were crying, women calling for their children or a parent, moms holding their crying and dying children in their arms. People who could not get to basements or bunkers died on the streets. We found children and women badly hurt, even burned to coal. We stayed with the hurt ones until help arrived. We started looking where basements might be to see or hear if there was any life, if there were people we could help to get them out.

We rolled stones and gravel away until the morning hours, hands and feet bleeding, but nothing was more important than to find hurt people or listening for people calling for help. It was so rewarding to help folks out of their basements, but sad finding so many of them dead. We sat there crying, and always, always asking the same question, "Why?"

In the morning we were looking for the train station. The trains were out in the city on empty tracks, as we were told. Trucks took people to the trains in time to wherever they needed to go.

It was a safe trip, but we were so tired and sad. Those pictures will stay with me for a long time, or forever. The country was beautiful. Our office was right on the Neckar River.

All of us got our work back, but lots of things changed. We were right. The company was an ammunition-making company. Everyone knew it was better not to talk about it.

There were some good and also bad months, but it also helped to remind myself—we live in a war. Sometimes I had food, but I often experienced hunger pain, mostly at night.

I remember walking to my barracks-home one early evening, thinking about what I could eat that night. I had one good-sized carrot, water and salt, making a healthy soup.

I could not believe my eyes. In the middle of the road lay a beautiful potato. I picked it up and said, "Thank you, Lord. You know I was hungry."

As I walked on, thinking about my soup, I thought, "What if a mom with children lost this potato? What if that Mom needs the potato more than I do?"

I walked back and put the potato in the middle of the road, just as I found it, sat down in the grass, cried a little and waited, hoping and praying no one would need the potato. I do not know how long I was there, but no one came. I took the potato, dreaming of a special good soup.

My recipe was simple: one good-sized carrot, water, one good-sized potato, salt….easy to put together and very, very good!

The next day, as so often, we heard the scary sound, "alarm". Everybody ran to the bunker. We only had a short way to the bunker, but enough to be safe from a bomb attack. My responsibility was to close the vault, which I did first, then started running.

By the wall across the street stood a young man. I wondered for a second why he did not go to the bunker. I was almost in the middle of the street, I heard an airplane. The young man called very loud, "Get down on the street now!" I did, and in a second he covered half of my body with his body, put his arm around me, pulled me very close to him and said, "Do not move. Do not move!"

The airplane came down and the bullets hit the street, not even one inch from my head to the feet. As the plane went up, the young man helped me up and said, "Now run to the bunker." I wanted to thank him, but he was not there anymore. There was no way he could hide. I never forgot, I thought very often about him.

He saved my life, and I wish I could have thanked him. Many, many years later, I told my husband about the happening. My husband looked at me and said, "Oh, Darling! Thank God. He sent a wonderful guardian angel to save your life." Even now, about seventy years later, my guardian angel is still in my heart.

There was a heavy bombing of Heilbron. After the bombing was over, we drove to see if we could help in any way, but what we saw was horrible. People could not reach a bunker. We found women and little children burned to coal lying on the street. We could not find our friends—they never returned.

It was unbelievable and heartbreaking to see women and children lifeless in the gravel and on streets. Trucks with lots of help, ambulances, and much more help came from all over. So many hands reached out to help, but there was very little anybody could do. We just stayed with the folks who were hurt until help came.

In the meantime, in another part of Germany, Mom, her four kids and grandparents kept walking. Sometimes they were lucky and were able to get a room or two in a farm home, good food and a bed. This did not happen very often, but Mom was thankful for every place they could put their tired bodies down. My sister told me that the pig stalls were the warmest. "Thank God we did not have to sleep outside at night," she said.

Cannon thunder came closer. That scary feeling was there, night and day. People were tired, hungry and scared. Mom and other people decided to settle down, just wait and see. The Russians were not far out and could very easily enter the town.

Mom stopped at a small farm house and asked the lady if she and her family could make their home for a while in the barn. The lady invited the family into her home, made a nice meal for all, let them clean up and told Mom to stay with her if she did not want to walk any more. I can see my Mom with her loving and thankful heart accepting the invitation. Other small families moved in. There was only peace for a short time. Grandpa died in his sleep, which was a blessing.

The Russians moved in, very loud, gunshots here and there. What is going to happen? People did not have to wait long. The Russians came into the village, screaming, shooting in the air, taking some homes from the people. Horrible days and nights followed.

The soldiers took the food away from the people and gave only small amounts to each family, not enough to live and not enough to die. Then the soldiers broke into homes asking for "frau" (women and girls), guns always pointed at the people. If one did not go willingly, they used them wherever they stood. Young women wore old-fashioned clothes and gave their faces an older look, but that did not help. There was often not even mercy for pregnant women.

They took children to the barn and used them, the kids were calling for Mom, screaming and begging to stop, and no one could help. Soldiers stood outside with guns, watching. The soldiers took watches, wedding bands, and everything shiny away from people.

One night three Russian soldiers broke into the home, grabbed my Mom, put her on the wall and said, "Down on your knees." Mom was raped. That was a sad day for the two kids to learn about life. My sister said, "Mom cried so bitterly, and we could not help because two Russian soldiers stood behind us with guns in our backs. We thought they were killing our Mom."

In those days, kids lived in a kid's world longer than in our time. From our home the soldiers got upstairs. A twelve-year-old was used, sobbing, crying, begging, "Let me go! I am only twelve years old." It did not matter. Those kids were marked for life. There was rape all over.

My sister told me a soldier came into our home, the other one outside watching. Mom, Grandma, and my two sisters got up quickly. Grandma stayed in the kitchen. The soldier said, "Frau", took my Mom's hand and pushed her down to the floor. Grandma came in, she spoke the Russian language very fluently and told the soldier to spare her daughter, and he said to Grandma, "I am here to please. Get out of here, old woman." Grandma went to the kitchen, got the iron frying pan, ran fast to him, hit him hard on the head. He passed out and Grandma said, "He came to be pleased. I pleased him." She opened the door and told the watchdog soldier to go fast and ask an officer to come, his friend got very ill. The soldier did, came back with the officer. Grandma sat next to that wounded soldier, but if he moved, she put the frying pan to work again. The official asked his people to take him out. He apologized to the family and praised Grandma. She thanked the official. Mom was saved, thanks to her Mom.

There was so little food. Hunger made my two sisters crawl at night to the Russian's camp to check the garbage cans to see if they could find some good bones for a soup.

The two kids left when everybody was sleeping. They did not expect Mom to hear them leave. Mom waited and worried. The two naughty girls returned, two happy faces that did not stop telling Mom about their happy adventure. They found very meaty bones.

"Don't worry, Mama. We knew what we had to do. We counted how long it takes for the light to reach us again. We were so careful. We knew where the soldiers sat together, drinking and laughing. You can wash all that very well and cook a good soup." Everyone in the house needed to know what the midnight excitement was, and the happy cooking started.

"This is wonderful," Mom said, "But no more. I was waiting for you, unhappy and scared"

Mom forbid the girls to go again, but both said, "Mom, that is better than sitting home, being hungry."

The next night those two little bad girls took off again. They found good bones in the garbage cans, but there was a kitchen window open. They smelled fresh-baked bread. No problem. The girls got in and each took one loaf of bread and were ready to leave when the light in the kitchen went on. The girls just stood there. Yes, their happy smile left for a little while.

A Russian officer watched the kids from the first day. He even saw them checking the garbage cans. He asked the girls why they were doing that, and they together, said, "We are hungry."

He said, "I am not angry with you." He took a large box, filled it with all kinds of good food. He followed the girls home, carried the heavy box into the home. He told Mom that he had three girls and was praying his three daughters would find a good soul if they were in need of help. Mom's girls went to the Russian soldier, put their arms around him and thanked him. Mom told him she was always praying for her five children. She would also pray for his three daughters. He thanked Mom and left. There are good people in our world, and there is love everywhere.

The folks had a few joyful days. No unwanted company, good food, but everyone had the same question, "How long can this last?"

Four days later everyone living in the village, young and old, had to gather in the next sixty minutes at a large empty field. That was not good. The soldier counted the people. After everyone was there, they were told to walk, the head and body bent down. If they straightened up, they would be shot. It was very hard, even more so for the elderly. They pushed the people like a herd of cows, Mom said. Grandma walked about three hours, then lost her will to live. She told Mom she was going to straighten up. Mom begged her to try a little longer. They would kill the rest of the family and other people, too.

"I do not want to lose my Mom this way, "she said. It was not much longer. The soldiers shot in the air, turned around and left.

People were hurting. They did not have shoes on, did not even have old clothing to wrap around their feet and not enough to stay warm at night. The three families from the house stayed together, knowing they could not return anymore. They decided to find the border to escape the Russians and get into the American part of Germany.

There were lots of people trying their luck. Walking through mine fields was a scary problem. Mom put long, heavy branches together, and each person took fifteen minutes to push those branches from side to side in front of everyone. How good was that idea? It was just a little hope and peace of mind.

It took months to reach the border. Walking and hiding became harder and harder. People were scared, hurting. They only traveled at night, hoping they would not be seen by the border guard. Finally they could see the border. One more night of walking and Mom saw the place she thought would be safe to get through.

The border was secured with electric fences. Everyone started digging to make a crawl space under the fence to the American side. Other families joined and worked hard together, only at night, hiding during the daytime. Finally the tunnel was large enough to crawl to safety.

A group of exhausted people cuddled up on the safe side of the fence and fell asleep.

Mom said that everyone thanked the Lord, and happy tears rolled down their cheeks. They needed to find the Red Cross to get some food and clean up.

All had a warm welcome at the Red Cross, a place to lie their worn bodies down, food and water.

Mom, Grandma and the kids rested, and then walked out of Berlin.

The family found a place to stay in a lovely small village. Mom hoped to find me by visiting the Red Cross again.

There were talks that the war may end in a few days. There was happiness and also sadness for almost every family because the war would not be over for many families.

Mom was celebrating Thanksgiving, being thankful that her two daughters, Elinor and Ruth, also Oma and the lady who gave them a home for a while were all safe. Mom and the girls went on their knees to thank the Lord Jesus for the love and protection they so much needed.

A very happy surprise for everyone! Hitler lost World War II. Thank God. An unforgettable wonderful day.

Part 3

After World War 2

Mom found my name at the Red Cross. It did not take long and Mom went on the road again. The children stayed in Grandma's care. Part of the way Mom could travel by train, also truck drivers stopped, and took people as far as possible.

A very happy day began. The doorbell rang. My adopted Mom (Mrs. Kraft) went to the door and a soft voice asked, "My daughter lives with you?"

Mrs. Kraft invited her to come in. I heard my Mom's voice and all I could say, "Mama, my Mama!" It was so good after so many years being in her arms again. I was praying for this moment. We only had one night and until noon the next day. Mom had the chance to go back with the same truck driver and also catch a train. Lots of happy tears were shed, but the parting was not so sad. It would take a while, but we would be together again.

Mom made it back to her family. Grandma, the kids and Mom had a lot to talk about, everyone happy, thinking it will not take too long and they will have a home again and praying that happy days will follow.

Mom, Grandma and the kids started planning the next trip to the south. That little hand wagon was packed again, but this time with some clothing bought from the money the Red Cross kindly donated, and some food. This trip can only be a happy walking trip because there was only money left for food and that was fine. They always had to ask for a place to stay for the night. People were helpful.

It took a long time, but one day a little hand wagon, pulled by my two sisters, with Oma sitting on top of it (she could not walk anymore) and Mama following in the back made the way to my adopted family.

It was very sad, a heartbreaking picture. I looked at my sisters, Grandma and Mom, but could not run to them and put my arms around them. Little sadness came over me, looking at my two sisters, not young kids anymore, beautiful blooming young women; my Mom, my best friend, looking at all the helpful people with thankful eyes; and Grandma waiting patiently for help to get off her not-so-comfortable hand wagon seat.

People knew they were my family and gave them a warm welcome. Our mayor gave all the help my family needed and more. Mom, Grandma, the kids and all their belongings had to be disinfected before they could come to Mr. and Mrs. Kraft's home.

Mrs. Kraft asked me to fix a meal for all of us. That I gladly did. Then a little voice from my Grandma, "ich bin so hungrig fur kartoffel"—(I am so hungry for potatoes). Mrs. Kraft said, "We have enough potatoes. Cook a large pot full."

"You dear Grandma", I thought. "How little you need to be happy!" That is my Oma.

In the between time, the mayor of our town got in touch with the mayor from a small village, mostly farmers, and found that there was a room with an outhouse, no running water, but not far from there an outside water pump. When my family heard the news, they could not have been more thankful and happy.

My sister said, "Mama, you told us we will have a house again and be happy, and we will find the rest of the family."

Mom said, "We will pray for that day."

I was very thankful for the love and help and for the most wonderful welcome my family received, and so was my family. "And now we will have a home— no more running and begging to find a place to rest," Mom said.

They were thankful to the mayor who gave a train porter for the family, also enough blankets to move to their first home. More than five years being homeless and on the road! Everything was so well done for my family, a bed for Mom and Grandma, lots of blankets and pillows for the girls. The mayor also gave Mama enough money so she could live without worry. Grandma sat on the bed, Mom and the two girls got on their knees, thanked the Lord for the new beginning, for all the people so willing to help in all those years, and for finding me. Two churches were very helpful, and also lots of people from the village. My sisters made good friends, Mom too. Both of my sisters started school and the three of them found the church. We believed in our prayers and talks with the Lord. We knew He will hear us and we greeted each day with love and thankfulness in our hearts.

Life was good to my family, good neighbors, good friends.

One day a delivery to Mom—a sewing machine on a stand, a gift from the village people, an undeniable joy. People brought work to Mom; even material Mom could use for my two sisters and also could make some birthday gifts for my sisters' friends. People always asked Mom how she wanted to be paid for the work she did for them...flowers, butter, eggs, potatoes, or money. We were happy, but missed Dad and my two brothers so much. We walked daily to the bus station to see if one of our three soldiers were coming home.

My 15 year old brother, Arno, was taken to the army. He had no training, never a gun in his hands or hanging over his shoulder, the uniform too large. He was a picture of a not-even-funny soldier with a gun hanging around his shoulder to the ground. He was wounded three times, was in different hospitals, and returned four-and-a-half years after the war. We loved our brother…a kind, loving and caring man.

My brother's wish was to become a forester. He loved trees, animals, flowers, and the feeling of peace walking through the forest. When we were children, we walked almost daily through a part of a large forest to find hurt deer, rabbits, or other wounded animals, took them home to our barn hospital to help them get back to the woods again. There were times the deer returned to the barn.

My brother's hurting body made him reach out to alcohol. Our brother lost his love for life. He never forgot his comrades and the little children and young kids on streets, homeless and dying.

I still feel the joy, thinking about walking with my brothers and sisters through the beautiful forest. My brother's dream never came true. He died at age 50.

My 13 year old brother, Horst, was outside when a truck came by. Two Russians grabbed my brother and dumped him just like other boys, age thirteen, fourteen or fifteen into a truck and took off. Mom looked all over for her son, but he was nowhere. About two months later, a Russian officer told Mom they took the kid to Siberia to work.

The heartache was almost too much for Mom. It never ended.

I walked to the bus station as always, hoping my brother would come home. One day a man came slowly along the street. He had no shoes on, just rags wrapped around his feet. Every step he took left blood on the asphalt. I thought I must help him. As he got close to me, he stopped, looked at me with sad eyes and asked, "Where is my Mom?"

I said, "I do not know where you Mama is."

"Don't you live with my Mom?"

"No, I live with my Mom."

"Where do you live?" he asked.

"Over there in that little house."

Then tears rolled down his cheeks and he said, "Don't you know me anymore? I am your brother."

We fell to our knees, crying, hugging. Then I said, "Let's go home. Mom and the girls and Oma will be so happy." That was a most wonderful day for all of us.

My brother told us that it was a sad trip to Siberia. The kids were crying for their moms. The Russians warned them to stop. If they did not stop, they got a bad hit with the hand-held side of the gun. Some passed out and were thrown from the truck to die. It was a long trip. Some of the kids died, my brother could not figure out why. Some got ill in Siberia and died. My brother said he wanted to come home. That was all he could think. He did what he was asked to do. Regardless of how good it was, it was not always good enough for the Russians, and he got paid with sticks and belts.

When my brother returned, he was very ill, his whole body filled with fluid, bleeding and pus-filled legs and feet. He asked me if he could take a bath. He was smiling when I told him,
"We do not live that fancy, but I will put a large bathtub in the kitchen. I will heat the water. It is large enough. You can sit in there, enjoy and love the luxury."

He was laughing. It warmed our hearts, and joyfully he said, "I forgot how wonderful love is!"

He asked me not to let Mom wash his back. He wanted me to do it. I found five welts across his back. I felt like crying out, and my brother said, "Do not stop your feelings. Cry if you have to." My brother returned almost five years after the war. He was eighteen years old.

It took more than a year for my brother to go out and look for work, and he also was able to go for a few years to school and became an auto-mechanic master. He worked and took also school at a hospital and became an ambulance driver for many years. He loved to help people. He then had an offer to become a trouble-shooter for a large car company.

My brother was a happy person, always helpful wherever help was needed. He had a wonderful personality.

One day, while he was an ambulance driver, his wife and three friends went on a shopping spree and drove along the beautiful Neckar River to a larger city. A car came around a corner, hit the women's car almost front-on and pushed the car down the little hill toward the Neckar River. The car was stopped by a tree. Somebody called the ambulance. My brother came. He called two more ambulances.

They found three very hurt women. They were taken to the hospital. My brother's wife was missing. My brother and his help looked all over, calling her name. Then my brother found her, half of her body lying in the river. She was just saved by a small tree branch lying in the river.

As he got her out, he noticed that the top of her head was cut off. He asked his ambulance friend to drive as fast as the car would go. She needed to be in surgery.

My brother called for another ambulance to come fast and bring a cooler with ice. He kept looking for the headpiece. It had to be there or fall into the Neckar River.

My brother said he just looked up and said, "Please, God." There in the tree hung the headpiece. He got it down. The cooler was not far from him, and he took off to the hospital, praying it would not be too late for the surgery.

The operation turned out perfectly, no one ever could see that there was a problem. My brother, the wonderful ambulance driver! The driver who caused the accident was heavily intoxicated and had to be taken to the hospital.

Papa was the only one missing. One of us always went to the bus station, hoping he would be there. He did not take the bus. He came by train to the city and walked for one hour.

More than five years after the war we had our Dad back, but he was not our Dad anymore.

He was an angry man, even hateful. We knew we had a very ill, broken in heart and soul, wounded Papa with us. We could see that he was in pain. His back and arms were full of red welts that sticks and belts must have been the pay in the Russian and Poland prison.

He was crying and screaming at night not to shoot the women and children. He held his hands in front of him as if he wanted to protect them. We lay awake at night, too scared to go to sleep.

We kids decided to take turns, each one of us watching for one hour throughout the night. We had less sleep, but more peaceful.

Mom asked Dad to see a doctor and he did, but found that there was not much he could do to help Dad. Hospitals were full with wounded soldiers. Doctors were needed, but Dad did not want another doctor or any help anymore. In each person he saw a bad soldier.

Our Dad was, beside other illnesses, mentally ill. Stress, anxiety, depression lived with him night and day. A sad way of life started for the whole family. I started believing Dad did not love us anymore. We still loved our Papa, even we could see the hate in his eyes when he looked at us.

He never asked us to do something for him. It was always a must, a command, and "do it now."

I started looking deeper into Dad's heart. He really did not know we were his children. Each time I walked by Dad, I said, "I love you, Papa." Sometimes I felt those hateful eyes, looking at me, and quite often, I saw him bending his head a little to the side, looking at me with different eyes, like wondering "Why is she so nice to me?"

We started getting ill. We did not have a life anymore. If Dad would only remember we were his family, we could at least put our arms around him for just a little while. I know our Dad did not ever want to live this life. He just could not get out of the misery. It was the war that made our Papa so ill.

I remember how sad it was sitting at the dining table saying grace, hoping we can enjoy our meal when Dad sat with us, but those hateful looks brought tears to our eyes, and so often we left the table hungry. We had our meal when Dad took his afternoon rest. It was not the meal we were longing for, it was his love we missed so much.

Was that our Dad? We asked that question so often. Every night I got together with my brothers and sisters to pray for our Papa. We could not give up on him, not lose the love for him. We believed God will hear our prayer. God is good.

We also were praying for Mom and us kids. We needed to stay strong and most of all, healthy. All of us felt a very ill sadness in us. We sure cried for God's help.

It was also very sad seeing my two brothers in pain and not being able to help. My sisters were wonderful, trying in every way possible to bring a little happiness to our two brothers by playing card games or whatever they could come up with to let them, even only for a while, forget the war and pain. We could not do anything for Papa. That was very hard on us. Stress, crying, screaming not to shoot the women and kids were still the five years World War II memories he could not forget.

It was not easy to even dream about a merry Christmas. It was a very cold winter day with a lot of snow. I went to the woods, walking around to look for a small tree which I thought would look lovely on the table

Decoration? I have to get Mama's help. Together we will find a way. Mom baked some cookies to hang on the tree. In the evening I told my sisters it would be nice if we had at least one candle on our tree, but I did not have ten pennies. Every penny was saved for food and medicine.

The next day my sisters went to some houses where elderly lived and asked if there was something they could do for them. The kids helped the elderly often and did not take any money. This time, they took the pennies and gave them a big thank you.

We were able to buy one Christmas candle. That made our tree complete!

Mom lit the candle. We sang "Stille nacht, heiliege nacht," except Papa.

We were still Papa's bad soldiers, but we loved him. We knew our love will make Papa well again, and life will fall into place again.

Mom tried to bring loving memories back, but they did not mean anything to Dad. Dad did not talk. We knew it would have never been that way if life had been normal. Dad would never have lost the love for Mom and his kids. Our doctor did not know how to help Papa. A Catholic priest offered help. He had some schooling in counseling and was willing to try. Dad did not feel that is important. We are not Catholic, but the young priest said, "The offer for help stands." We were thankful.

Mom said, "The war made Papa forget how wonderful our life was. He will not listen to anyone who is trying to help. Now I have to try something that will hurt all of us or make life better."

One morning Dad went to the Post Office. That is what he told Mom. Mom packed his old suitcase with his belongings, put $50 between the suitcase and handle and set the suitcase outside of the door. She locked the door and window, went upstairs, opened the window and waited for Dad's return.

I stood behind her, begged Mom not to do that, it is our Papa.

"Yes," Mom said. "It is Papa, but it is not our Papa anymore. I will not let my children get ill, too."

"Are you sad, Mama?" I asked.

"Yes", she said. "It is not easy. I love your Dad. I love my family so much. With God's help, I got my kids home. I pray the Lord will hear me again. Papa is very ill, demanding, angry, and so hateful. He is still in the war, but as hard as it is, we cannot let that happen much longer. Do not worry. I will not let our ill Papa be homeless. If this does not work, we will and must find another way. Let us pray for Dad, ask the Lord to help him. We love and need him."

Dad was at the door, looking at his suitcase. He looked up to Mom and said, "Why, Mama?"

Mom said, "Papa, I love you very much and your children want Papa back. They want to feel Dad's arms around them. They want a smile, a hug, praise, but you treat your children like bad soldiers. You have two sons here. Both came out of the war, both very ill. Only one little smile from you would bring joy to their lives, and it would be the most powerful medication. Love is powerful, Dad. We have an angry Dad in our lives and that cannot go on any longer. The Catholic priest offered help, you do not take it. I want my children well, Papa, but that is, with the way you treat them, not possible. Your promises are not good enough."

Dad looked at Mom and said, "Mama, open the door one more time. I will try hard to do what you ask me to do. I will go to the doctor. I will take the medication."

Mom asked, "What about the priest?"

Dad said, "I will see the priest whenever he wants to see me."

" Promise me that you will try to be good to the children"

"Yes, I will," Dad said. "Open the door, Mama, one more time, please."

Mom did. I went to the door with Mom, wanted to give Dad a little hug, but he walked out of my way. That was so painful.

Dad kept his promises, when Mom was around he was a little nice to us kids. When he knew or thought Mom was not home, we were still his bad soldiers. Dad did not know what a good spy Mom was. I did not either.

One day at the dinner table, we were done with our meal. Mom asked us kids to please find another place to go. Dad would like to talk to Mom. We left, but Dad was surprised. He did not ask for a conversation. She just wanted Dad to stay, not jump up and walk away.

I learned from Mom. This time I was a little spy. I heard Mom asking Dad, "What do our children mean to you. Are they still your bad soldiers"

Dad started crying. For the first time, Dad took Mom's question to heart. Mom did not say more. It was not easy for Mom, either.

The priest and Dad saw each other almost daily, and also started taking long walks together. When Mom was baking bread, Dad invited the priest for breakfast. Flour, butter, marmalade or jelly was often Mom's pay for the sewing work she did. Those were thankful hours we had together.

Dad started taking his afternoon naps in the small woods not far from the village. We still kept watching

Dad's activities and often followed him. Yes, all of us became little spies.

Dad decided to visit the woods again. My sister Elinor followed him. It was easy to do because there was the corn-field along the street almost up to the woods. Dad went into the woods, sat down on a tree, and after a while lay down and fell asleep.

My sister went to him, lay beside Papa and put her arm around him. She fell asleep also. When Dad awoke, she right away sat up and they just looked at each other.

Dad helped her up. They stood there for a while. Then Dad took her hand and said, "Let's go home." They did not talk, just walked. How happy my little sister's heart was!

When both got home, Mom put her arms around Papa and said, "That is a beautiful beginning'", and she praised and hugged my sister.

Papa started talking to his sons, even hugging. Slowly, but honestly, love returned to our home. Dad asked us children to walk with him. He remembered the hard time he gave us and was very sad about it. He did not know how to stop or get out of the misery. He said he did not see our faces, just uniforms.

So much changed in our life. Dad took still all the help he could get. We were more than thankful to our priest. Dad loved him like he loved his own sons, and he became a loving member of our family. We never lost our love and respect for each other.

Life got better day by day. All of us were so thankful our prayers were answered. About one year later, Papa started working for a sauerkraut business. He got his own little office outside, checked every person for the company's identity card. He loved his job and made good friends.

Mom got the praise from all of us. Her happy outlook on life, great attitude and her steadfast faith did provide each one of us with the strength to endure and overcome.

Even after almost eighty-nine years, I love you, Mom.

Now is the time to tell you a little about my Dad's love for my Mom. Dad was an early riser. He loved to see the sunrise, watch the birds, walk along fields and woods, and watch the deer. In the summer time, every Saturday, Papa picked a bouquet of wild flowers for Mom and laid them next to Mom's pillow. Mom loved flowers.

In the wintertime, rain or shine, Papa made his morning walks. Mom needs flowers, but....

Papa found some lovely-looking twigs and made a beautiful bouquet, put it next to Mom's pillow. When Mom awoke and saw the branches, she said, "Not in our bed, Papa!"

Dad heard her, came in and said, "Mama, I would buy you the most beautiful flowers, but that is just not possible. I thought I would bring the iron kettle to the patio. You could fill it with the twigs, and for Christmas, I will put lots of lights on the twigs. That would be very beautiful."

When Mom told me the story, she was not pleased with all the wood Dad brought home. She knew Dad wanted to please her and that made Mom like the twigs. (She burned a lot!)

That twigs bouquet became the talk of the little town. The lights in the branches looked almost as great as the early morning sun. How little it takes to please! That was my Dad's love for my Mom.

A lovely, but also sad story comes to mind, a story about George, our rabbit, and Papa. We were thankful to a farmer who rented us an old house with three bedrooms, two upstairs that gave the girls and boys their separate bedrooms, also a kitchen and living room. A part of the living room became Grandma's room which she loved dearly. Not to forget a lovely outhouse! Next to our house stood the preacher's beautiful house and across the street, our church.

The farmer let us use an old shed. My sisters cleaned it up, washed the window and asked lots of people in the village if they would like to get rid of old wooden boxes. Our neighbor farmer put doors with screens on, and my sister started raising rabbits. She went every day to find rabbit food and often her friends and retired people brought rabbit food to her.

She sold them to very low income elderly people very, very reasonable. How sad it was for us, standing in front of a grocery store, counting the pennies. I praised my sister for the wonderful labor of love.

One day a rabbit-mom gave birth to a bundle of little ones. She started to kill them all. My sister came in time to only get one away from her, took it into our house, and made a warm bed for that little one in the "back-ofen" (oven).

My sister cared for that little rabbit night and day, and she was also a good teacher. That little rabbit became a part of our family. We never had a toilet problem with him. He knew how to ask when he needed to go outside.

My sister named her rabbit George. He did not like Grandma. He waited for her to get out of bed and bit her in the heel. Not serious, but that made Grandma very angry, and each time she was ready to get out of bed in the morning, we heard her calling, "Will somebody come and get that rabbit out of here?"

We thought that was funny, but it was not—and today I think about it and a feel a little sad. Grandma was too old for that kind of loving the two-year-old rabbit gave her.

It was a very beautiful sunny Sunday morning. We got ready to go to church, when Dad said he would like to stay home and start the meal. It was nothing new to us, Dad loved to do that.

Coming home from church, the table was set. Dad said, "You can come to the table as soon as you are ready."

Washing hands, we went to the table, Dad said grace. Dad brought first the spazle (home-made noodle) Mom made a day before. Then the vegetables, and the last dish was the meat and gravy.

The excitement stopped. All eyes were on the meat and gravy, even Papa's.

With teary eyes, my sister looked at Dad, asking, "Papa, did you cook George?"

Papa thought, his heart is going to stop. After a while he said, "I know that you did not have a good meal for a long time. Every special meal you were able to cook went to your brothers and Papa. I know we needed that, but so did you. The rabbit's life would not have been for long anymore....." Dad could not talk anymore.

He called the preacher, asking him if he would like a dish of meat and gravy. The preacher was happy! Dad took it over to him. Papa turned around to walk out when the preacher asked, "Martin, is that George?"

Dad did not answer, did not come home, either. He took a long walk.

When he returned, we went to Dad, telling him that we loved him and that we knew he did that out of love for his family. We were sad, we loved George, but the love for our Dad was stronger.

Some wonderful years went by, then my Dad got very ill—cancer. By this time I lived with my husband in America.

My husband thought it would be good for me to be for a while with my parents.

I prepared for my trip, also cooked different meals to put a one-month supply in the freezer so my husband would have a daily home-cooked meal.

My husband joined me one month later. Dad always said not to think about illness, even wonder when the Lord will call his name. Let the time we have together be happy.

We tried to be cheerful, played a lot of games and had lovely walks together. Dad was very interested in all our lives, especially about my life, and was pleased to hear that our church is a part of our lives.

It was time for us to return to America. We left a very ill Dad and a sad Mom. We said our "goodbye"--it was painful. Dad did not want me to come home for his funeral. He wanted me to keep the memories we made together in my heart. Papa was right. When I think about the good times we had together, I am smiling.

Just a few months later, Dad needed to check into the hospital. Mom did not feel so good, and Dad asked her to stay home. He would be happy to get a bed and rest. He kissed Mom goodbye and told her when she is ready to come to heaven, to call the Lord, ask Him to take her home. Dad said, "I will wait for you." Dad did not die very happy, he was thinking about his young soldiers who had to give their lives in WWII. He lay there with teary eyes when Mom said, "I love you Papa. Reach out to the Lord. Go with Him." Dad died happy, and we are thankful.

Every Saturday my sister took Mom to the cemetery to put a rose on Papa's grave. Not even a year later, Mom took ill. We believe she was ready to be with Papa, but the Lord was not ready for her. My sisters told Mom we love her and want her with us a little longer.

My sister took Mom to the store as on every Saturday to get a rose for Papa, but this time Mom said, "Bring only one single daisy."

My sister just said, "Mama, I am not going to buy only one daisy!"

Mom said, "That is OK. I will go."

My sister told the saleslady Mom's wish, and the lady said, "I will do anything for your Mom."

At the graveside, Mom held the beautiful daisy in her hand. She was lost in her own thoughts. My sister was quiet, wondering about the daisy. Mom put the daisy on Dad's grave and said, "Papa, you do not keep your promise, you do not listen to me! No more roses, Papa! Daisies!"

My husband and I took another vacation to be with Mom. It was a special and happy time we had together. We visited places Mom and Dad loved to go to. We drove to the place where my husband and I met each other for the first time, places that did not tire Mom out but made wonderful memories. We visited castles where wheelchairs were available. We had a precious time with Mom. The month went fast. The thought of our parting again filled my heart with sadness.

The day for another goodbye—Mom held me in her arms and said, "This is the last time we will hold each other. I love you very much and I am thankful for the love you give so freely to your parents, brothers, sisters, and everyone who touches your life."

Mom said, "I know you have to go now. Take my love with you, and please, do not come to my funeral. Keep our memories we made together in your heart, and thank the Lord for all the blessings He is granting you." A big hug and kiss for Mom.

She put her arms around my husband and said, "Son, I love you and thank you for being so good to my daughter. God bless you, my Son." He held Mom and did not want to let go. My husband turned around and walked away. He loved Mom. Sad hearts, tears, our last goodbye from our Mom.

We went back to America. Sadness was in our hearts and it stayed with us for a long time. That was a very sad flight home.

We called Mom once a week and I am thankful for that.

Another year went by and Mom was ready to move into the hospital. She was tired and ready to reach out to the Lord. The doctor asked Mom if she had a problem, and Mom said, "I am ready to go to Papa."

The doctor had known Mom and Dad for a long time.

Mom wanted to thank everyone and asked the doctor if he could ask the cleaning women, doctors and people who helped Mom to come to her room. Mom's kids were with her. It was a special time for Mom, and she thanked everyone for taking care of Dad and Mom.

Everyone gave Mom a hug. Then she said to my sisters that she would love to be covered with her comforter in her casket. My younger sister asked, "Why, Mama?

Mom said, "I am sure it is very cold down there."

I believe she just said that to make everyone smile, not cry. Then she said that it was time for her. She kissed the girls and told them, "It is OK to cry for a little while, but I want you to be just as happy as your Mama was. I was blessed with five wonderful children and a good husband. Make that your life, too." The children kissed her and thanked her for being a wonderful, loving mom.

She asked everyone to leave her. She wanted to be with Jesus. That short walk leaving Mom was so hard. Everyone stood outside when the doctor said, "I hear your Mom." He opened the door and said, "Bertel?"

Mom looked at my sisters and said, "Would you be so nice to put my good walking shoes on my feet?"

My sister said, "Mom, you do not need your walking shoes."

And Mama said, "I sure do. Papa was not always perfect. The Lord might have sent him the long way to Heaven, and I have to find him." We promised that her walking shoes would be on her feet. Mom said, "Thank you," and the door closed again.

Everyone was talking, crying and smiling behind the door. Mom called again. My two sisters opened the door and asked Mom if she forgot something. "Yes," she said, "would you put a bouquet of roses in my arms? I would like to take them to Papa."

"Yes, Mom. We'd love to do that." The love my two sisters felt that minute for Mom and Dad was heartwarming. The door closed for the last time. Mom closed her eyes.

She always gave joy and love, and she left this world happy. We love you, Mom. Mom had many friends. Her funeral room was a flower garden. She loved flowers.

It took a lot of headache and tears to talk about my family, even our lives together. Living my young life without Mama and Papa was not easy, but I sure tried the best I could.

The factory moved to a little town near Insbruck. We were on our own. When we heard the war could come to the end. Soldiers and people from our factory started fires on the streets and burned their uniforms, papers that would show their identity. They even grabbed our purses or whatever we had in our hands and burned all papers. We had no identification anymore. There were so many mixed feelings, almost scary.

The soldiers went to homes, asking people if they could give them some men's clothing. Some people were not willing to do some, but some men took what they needed.

We young women were taken to a school house to spend a few nights. Everything was ready for us, even good food. We had a restful night. The thought that this could be the end of the war gave everyone a happy feeling.

Late in the afternoon of the second day, we were sitting on the floor, asking each other about our dreams. We heard loud laughing, singing and yelling. A truck full of men, in uniforms private clothing, jumped from the truck and ran across the yard to our school building.

We were so scared, locked doors and windows. The men behaved like animals, broke doors and windows.

My girlfriend and I went to the bathroom and climbed out of a little window, running and hiding behind a large tree. We ran for our life; that was our only chance.

We heard our friends screaming, "No! No! Please!" and "Do not hurt me!" They raped the girls, then made them take off all their clothing and different men raped them again.

After the animals left, we returned. Our friends lay on the floor, crying, hurting, scared. We sat down with them, but there was really nothing we could do or say to ease the pain. To help only a little, the women took their showers and went to bed. My girlfriend and I pushed tables and chairs in the broken doorway and covered the windows with blackboards as good as possible.

We aimed our ears to the outside, but the rest of the night was quiet.

Some women came after midnight and asked us to go to bed. Yes, we were tired and not used to that kind of work, but that was all we could do for our friends. We went to bed, but still heard our friends crying.

The next day started very sad for all of us. The women were scared---what if?? There was no answer. All we could do is pray with our friends that this rape will not bring more trouble. At noon we went downtown. The people hung white flags out of windows, telling the American soldiers, "We are giving up."

People called out of the windows, telling us the war was over. Happy tears ran down my cheeks and I cried loud out, "Mama, I am still alive, please find me!"

It was a sad, but still a happy day. We heard where the American soldiers were and that they were coming our way. The idea that the American soldiers are on the way to our town took my fear away.

The streets were empty, people asked me to go into a house, that the soldiers would shoot me, but I did not want to hear that.

I asked myself, "How long it will take until our family will find each other?" But I know we will be together again. I never before experienced my heart full of happiness and sadness together. I loved that thought that there will be peace again and hope for a better life.

I prayed my family would find each other and find me. I thought about my brothers and sisters, how much would I have loved watching them growing up, being there for them, Dad and Mom, who tried to guide us through good and bad times and loved us unconditionally.

The war was over, the fighting stopped. No more bomb attacks, no more running to the bunkers. What a feeling of relief!

But were the "battles" over? For many families the fear of the unknown, the anxiety of a search for loved ones, the need to find a place to live, and'/or just the courage to cope with our war-torn world were almost impossible obstacles.

Towns were bombed out, buildings lay in rubble, and commerce was at a stand-still. People were left without shelter or food, happy to find a place to rest, if only for one night.

I ask myself how long it would take until our family would find each other. My heart was filled with happiness and sadness. I loved the thought that there would be peace again and hope for a better life. I prayed my family would find each other, and find me.

I thought about my brothers and sisters, about how much I would have love watching them growing up, being there for them. I thought about my Mom and Dad, who tried to guide us through good and bad times and loved us unconditionally.

Hitler's war was over, but for so many people, the war is just beginning. So many Moms and their kids homeless. I was one of them, and also my family. What about the elderly? Orphans? Our soldiers? And I am thinking not only of Germany. Many Moms cried about their children, husbands, and/or loved ones. Why? Everyone needs to be happy again, but how many years will it take in our war-torn Germany?

I watched the beautiful winding road, almost knowing that is the road where I will see the first American tanks.

Mid-afternoon we heard the sound of heavy tanks coming down the winding road. The tanks were decorated with the American flag flying high. So many wishes, so many dreams touched my heart as I was waiting till the first tank rolled into the little town.

It was the sound of peace and a new start of life, and I will greet this day with love in my heart. Like a little kid, I waved welcome to the soldiers, tank by tank, and they returned my greeting.

The tanks rolled to a large field behind the school building. People from our company and other places were asked by loudspeaker to come to the field where the tanks stood. The call was not for people living at the village. American soldiers stood in line and handed each one of us a food package, and I got an extra block of chocolate. I was the kid in our group.

That night, men and women had to stay at that school. Doors and windows were repaired and inside everything in order. It still was an uncomfortable feeling. We got good sandwiches, hot water for tea and coffee, cookies, and chocolate. We had a good night's rest.

The next day trucks were lined up, four for men, one for women. We heard that we would be taken to Heilbron to a prison camp. We were not scared. The war was over, it cannot be that bad anymore. After a long drive, the trucks stopped. The women's truck was the last one.

Behind a very high fence stood a lot of men, old and young, and women. They were waving, laughing, and calling something we did not understand.

I sat on the end of the truck, had my legs hanging down. I had leather boots on up to my knees. Those were all the shoes I had. It was uncomfortably warm. An African-American, a gun on his shoulder, came to our truck, looked at my legs and asked in very good German, "How long have you had your boots on?'

I told him that I did not know, but for quite a while, because I could not take them off. He touched my legs with both hands, looked at me and said, "We have to take the boots off." He walked away and came back with a bag, took a knife out and started working. When he had come about six inches down, my leg jumped almost out of my boots and did not have a good color. He had a hard time taking the rest off. He took the other boot off. I did not believe that those were my legs and feet.

He said something about gangrene. I did not know what he was talking about. Another soldier came, looked at my legs. They were talking in English, and then he left.

I got a shot. He explained why. I had to take pills and whatever he did, he explained. He made me stand up and take a few steps. The soldier walked away for a little while, came back and gave me a pair of his socks and said, "I'll check on you later."

It did not take too long before he returned, checked my legs, then said, "Whoever wants to walk away, do it now. I will turn my back to you."

I said to my girlfriend Elisabeth, "Let us go." I am scared to be behind that fence." Just the two of us decided to walk. Before we left, I went to the soldier to thank him and we left.

It was a very hard walk. The streets were still not in the best order from the bombing. We had to ask people if they would let us stay for a night. We had to be off the street at 5:00 p.m. as I remember. We were lucky. A family invited us to stay for the night, gave us something to eat, and we were thankful. Our plan was to walk to Neckarzimmern.

We started walking. It was not easy without shoes, but I was so thankful to the American soldier. I walked mostly in grass that made my little problem better. We walked for a while, then heard the sound of a car, an American truck. We jumped in a ditch, lay straight down, hoping they would not see us. We were so scared. The truck stopped where we were lying and we heard a voice, "Come." Two soldiers, African-Americans, were in the truck. One got out, took my hand and helped me into the seat next him. He then helped Elisabeth into the back of the truck with the other soldier. We drove about thirty minutes when the soldier turned into a small driveway. There was an evergreen orchard. Beyond the evergreen woods was a destroyed farm house. The soldiers were very friendly. If we only could understand each other!

I was so scared I could hardly walk. "Elisabeth ", I said, "I want to die."

"That is not going to work", she said. My girlfriend was 1 1/2 years older than I.

Everyone got out of the truck. The soldiers had a large blanket which they laid in the grass. I froze.

The soldiers went back to the truck and brought out a good-sized wooden box, put it on the blanket and got a lot of sandwiches and good food out of the box, even paper plates and cups. They asked us to eat as much and whatever we wanted, and the soldiers ate too.

I said, "Elisabeth, eat slow. That is probably our last meal." Each time I said something to my girlfriend, the soldiers looked at each other and smiled. I was never so scared in my life. We had about thirty minutes, then they started putting the food back into the box, folded the blanket and everything got back into the truck

I felt a little better. The soldiers asked us where we would like to go. We told them, and they said that they could take us only so far, and then would have to let us walk again.

I do not know how long we drove. When the soldiers stopped, they took a hand wagon from some piece on the truck, put the box with food in it, said in a broken German, "God bless you. Hope you find a place to stay." They asked, "Where will you start to find a place?"

I said, "The mayor's office." That was the best. I gave both of them a hug, so did Elisabeth, and we parted with love in our hearts for two African-

American gentlemen. We felt loved by two soldiers from another world. They knew we were scared, but I wanted to let those soldiers know that we were thankful. They turned around and left, and we went our way.

We walked into Neckarzimmern mid-afternoon. That gave us a little feeling of home.

We got to the mayor's office asking if we could have some help finding a place to stay for a night or two. The mayor sent me upstairs to a family, and my friend Elisabeth to the Baron's house next to the mayor's office. She had permission to move into a separate room with a bathroom. The Baron family gave her all she needed and she could stay as long as she wanted.

My family upstairs, Mr. and Mrs. Kraft, said I could stay for one or two days until their daughter returned from England. I was so thankful. A quick shower and a bed and I slept one night and half a day. When I opened my eyes, a couple was sitting next to my bed, smiling and saying they thought I did not want to wake up any more. She gave me one of her robes, asked me if I wanted to clean up a little. There was even a toothbrush for me. She asked me to come to the kitchen when I was done. She made a little soup and sandwich.

We talked, and it felt as if we knew each other for a long time. The lady worked at the Mayor's office and he was a teacher. The clothes I had on my body were washed and in my room. Both had to go to work. They gave me the time when both of them would be home, asked me to enjoy the day, and said if I had a question to come to the Mayor's office. I had not done any housework for so many years, so I cleaned the kitchen and took another rest. I was not tired, I just had not had a bed for a long time.

I went down to the office and asked Mrs. Kraft if she would let me cook the meal for the evening. She asked me if I could cook. I would love to.

After two days I said to Mr. and Mrs. Kraft, "I will go out and find a place to stay ", and both said if I wanted to, I could stay with them as long as I wanted, and that I was welcome. I really believe the Lord Jesus held His hands over the family Kraft and me.

About eight or ten days later, two African-American soldiers came to the Mayor's office asking if two young women were asking for a place to stay. Mrs. Kraft called me to come down to the office. Those two men were so happy that we found a place, and told the Mayor, who spoke English, that they were very happy to help two scared kids. There are wonderful people in this world. One of them was a lawyer from Chicago, the other one a businessman. That is all we heard from the mayor.

God was good to me. My adopted parents, Mr. and Mrs. Kraft, loved me like they loved their daughter. We had four happy years together. I found good work too far away to stay with the family, but I visited them as often as I could.

I remember the beautiful village of Neckarzimmern where I found love and happiness again. The village had only one main street, small side streets and a winding road that ran through vineyards and to a castle, Burg Hornberg. His little village had two lovely old churches. The largest buildings in this town were the Baron's private home and the Mayor's office with the upstairs apartment where my adopted parents, their daughter and I lived. A guesthouse which was well cared for was a family business. A beautiful, old, old tree stood near the main street with a bench under it. It looked like the elderly held their meetings in the morning under the shady tree, lighting their pipes, talking and laughing, a lovely picture to remember.

There were vineyards on hills up to the castle, which was a lovely place to visit. From the castle you could see the winding Neckar River and some small villages along the river. The food and service at the castle was first class.

Across the street from the Mayor's office were a little park and gardens. That area was used to build a prison camp where prisoners of war were housed. It was comfortable and well-managed. There were good relationships among the camp personnel, the town, and the prisoners. The prisoners were taken for swims and church services. Food was very good, cooked at the camp. Beyond the gardens and houses was the beautiful Neckar River.

My adopted parent's daughter and I swam, as soon as weather permitted, in the clean river.

One day an American soldier came with a number of prisoners for a swim. It was a normal practice for us girls to dive off the dam and swim under water as long as possible. This day an American and other soldiers watched me dive, became worried when I stayed too long under water, and sent two German prisoners to rescue me. I was pulled out and scolded by them, as if I were a naughty child.

I felt good—someone cared!

When we reached the shore, I discovered my nose was bleeding. The American soldier smiled and gave me his beautiful ironed handkerchief. I thanked him and thought, "If I could, I would marry him."

A few girls and boys met in the evenings at the Mayor's courtyard. I played the accordion and we were singing. We were very good, true friends. Along the street came an American soldier. It was the one who gave me his hanky. He stopped at the gate. One of the boys said, "He might be lonely, so far away from home. I will open the gate and ask him to join us."

He came every night. We were waiting for him. I introduced Jack to my adopted family. They invited him for the evening meal which I had to cook and even bake bread. Everything went fine and excitement made everything right.

My adopted family enjoyed my friend very much. I knew right then the seeds of friendship had been planted. We did indeed become good friends. He was a caring, kind and generous person, and he was loved by the village people. He especially gave attention to the children and elderly.

By this time I knew the love had blossomed in my heart. But how long will, or can this last, because he is an American soldier. In my heart, I believed that this dream will someday become reality.

He was like a son in my adopted parent's home. He was loved. Four months later he had to leave

Germany right away and go back to America. No explanation.

A little world fell apart for all of us. He gave me his picture, but left a sad heart behind.

We stood at the window to wave goodbye to him. The car stood on the street, but our American soldier was not there. I walked down the stairs, he was not there. I heard a sad sound and looked around the entry. There he was sitting, with teary eyes. He said, "I love the family very much and I love you, but I do not know what my life will be. I will write to you." He held me in his arms, turned around and walked away.

A sad parting. I waited for just a little note, asking myself, "Why does he not even send a little message?" I was hurt. My adopted family, who loved him very much, believed that something must have happened. That was not our American friend we loved very much. But, as always, heartache is the price we pay for love.

Three years later the first letter came to my adopted family, asking for me. We learned that he was taken to a hospital where he had to spend one year with tuberculosis. His mom, a preacher, and the Lord Jesus gave him the strength to get well again, well, as good as ever possible.

Then trying to find work, starting college, and still mending, it was hard for him to reach any serious decisions. Tuberculosis is a serious illness and can take years to heal, or was almost impossible 70 years ago. I am sure it was not an easy street for my friend to walk on.

We started writing, he in English, I in German. I could not read his letters. I do not know how many German words he still knew from staying in Germany.

We wrote to each other for thirteen years, then a letter came to tell me he would be in Bremerhafen on the ship MS-Berlin, if I could be there to meet him. My girlfriend of five years asked me if I wanted company. I was pleased.

Love, joy, and fear were in my heart. Will he still be the gentle, caring, loving person I loved so dearly? People started coming from the ship. I saw Jack, he looked a little older. I had the picture of him the way he looked thirteen years ago, plus the three years we did not hear from each other. Well, I got older, too, thinking will he still love me?

I said to my girlfriend, "There is Jack!" and she said, "I want him. I will fight for him." Knowing my friend, that is what she will do. I just said to her, "If he wants you, if he loves you, you can have him. I will never fight for love. I want unconditional love or nothing." End of conversation.

I walked towards Jack and found myself in his arms. Yes, he is the same loving man he was.

We had three months together. Our conversations were only with help from dictionaries. Finally we were able to get married.

We celebrated our wedding with our family, Mom and Dad's side and a few friends. It became a very special day for all of us. A day before our church service we had to get married in the courthouse. The Judge asked me if Jack understood some German. "Yes, he does," I said. The judge left for a while, my brother and girlfriend stood beside us when my soon-to-be-husband asked me, "When do I say, 'Yes, I do?"

"To make sure all goes fine, when the Judge asks you, I will touch your foot and that will be your time."

"OK", he said. The room was very beautiful with one large bouquet of flowers on a small table and one on the desk. The judge came in, everything went fine. I was so excited, but nervous. The judge was still talking about love, praise, and understanding when I touched my almost-husband's foot, not willingly, and he said, "Yes, I do. I love her."

The judge was laughing out loud, and said, "You are a good man. You do not need to hear more from me."

He married us. Then we said our vows at the church, which was just as lovely.

Three days after our wedding, my husband had to return to America to begin his new work. I could not go with him. I had no identification, everything was accepted on trust. I worked in the real estate business with an architect until I was able to go to America.

Four years later, a long but positive waiting time, we knew we would be together. Finally I followed my husband. A new beginning in a different world, a new language, a different life, but a very good life.

I was sad to leave my parents and the rest of the family again, but Mom made it easy for me again, and said, "You are my daughter and I know you will bloom where you are planted. You will be with your husband and you know that the two of you plan on coming home once a year. Make a good life for the two of you, and be happy."

My first visit to America was exciting, the first time in an airplane, looking out of the window, watching the clouds and gorgeous sunsets and sunrises, the most wonderful picture ever, the large airport in

Chicago, and my husband waiting for me. It was like a dream.

January, a very cold day, we were on the way to Iowa. It would have been a lovely drive in the summertime. All I could see were very large fields, large and small farms and freezing cows outside. I felt so bad for the cows and tears rolled down my cheeks. I turned away, did not want my husband to see my tears. He must have felt that I was troubled. He put his hand on my hands and said, "It is OK, dear heart."

Yes, it was OK. "I just have to learn about life in Iowa."

America and the people grew closer to my heart. Friends came with dictionaries in their hands to visit. We visited my parents and the rest of the family once a year. My husband was loved by my parents and families.

Thanksgiving today, the year 2013. I count my blessings, and the reasons to be thankful. I think about my parents who put the seeds of love and caring in our hearts. I thank my brothers and sisters for the love they had and have for each other, for the Lord Jesus, who saved my family's lives so very often, for guiding and loving me and helping me grow up at a time when I needed my parents the most.

I thank my friends for the love, understanding and encouragement I needed almost daily, and I am very thankful to my husband. He gave me a home, a great life, his unconditional love, and I love Iowa. I love America.

I am now 89 years old. I am thankful the Lord granted me a life with lot of love and happiness. There were scary days, sadness and tears, but that is, I believe, for all of us a built-in part of life.

I have seldom felt how great it is to be a child since I was six years old. I remember how happy I was when I was able to play with my brothers, sisters, and other children outside, without being scared that somebody could stand around the corner and take me away.

Mom and Grandma from another family were often watching over us. We did not need, and did not have, fancy or bought toys. A ball or two would do the trick. Running, hiding, just playing kept us happy. But since Dad refused to become a Hitler supporter, our whole little world started falling apart.

I remember my two little sisters, three and four years old, walking across a farmer's empty car-park to a large barn. My mom and other women were helping the farmer (a big Nazi supporter) piling straw, which came from the fields. Everybody needed the earnings. Mom saw her two kids and was ready to come down from the straw pile to see if they needed help when the farmer's woman ran to the children, hit them with her hands on the head and back and screamed, "Get off my farm!"

Mom could not be fast enough getting to the children. When the woman saw my Mom, she started running to her house and locked the door. My two sisters just wanted to tell Mama not to worry, that they both will be in the neighbor's home, eating and playing there until Mom came home. The neighbor's grandma watched the children as they walked to Mom.

It was sad that even the children had to feel and experience oppression and hurt.

Since I am slowly coming to the end of my writing, I am remembering that my new life in America has given me, and others, some moments of misunderstanding and laughter.

I am remembering a beautiful sunny day. My husband asked me if I would like to keep the car, a convertible, for the day so that I could get to know the city and surroundings—a great idea. I took my husband to work. On my way back, I ended up on a side street, a small road going to a main street. The music playing, I was singing and behind me I saw a police car, red lights flashing, sirens loud. I drove as fast as possible to the right, made sure he could pass me, but he did not. I drove faster, thinking he was in a hurry. I guess the police and I were not happy with each other. I stopped the car, jumped out and went to the police car. The car window was down and I said, "What are you doing? I gave you enough room to pass me. You did not. I thought you were in a hurry and drove faster, but I could not go faster on this street. Don't do that anymore. You know, I was happy and I want to stay that way. Auf Wiedersehn! (goodbye!)" I went to my car and drove home. The police car did not move. As I think about it today, I bet he had a good laugh.

It was time to pick up my husband. He asked me if I had a good day, and talked about little things.

I had a meeting that evening in the Howard Johnson Restaurant. My husband offered to join me. As we got into Howard Johnson, there was a table with five policemen and one of them hollered, "There she is!"

I just waved at them and went to the meeting room. I was just a few months in this country. I sat down next to my husband. He just looked at me, shook his head, and smilingly said, "Darling, darling, already the police are getting to know you."

Well, I thought, that is OK, too.

I wonder if this friendly police officer will have the chance to read this. I think about our conversation so often. He did not say anything—I wonder what he was thinking.

And then there are the language problems!

The phone rang. I answered, and there was Ms. Grau, the lady we bought our first beautiful Cedar Falls house from. Ms. Grau and her housekeeper came with the package, even though they planned to move into a smaller, but beautiful home. At the time when we had the buying conversation with the owner, the four of us had the feeling of belonging, the feeling of a true friendship.

Their new home was not ready to move into. Ms. Grau asked us if we would let them stay with us for about three weeks. My husband and I did not mind helping out. We were happy together and asked them to use the whole house and feel at home.

The housekeeper, Helen, was more than happy. When she heard that my husband loved pies, she baked every day another one to please him. We played together, took short trips together, and stayed fast friends.

One day Ms. Grau asked, "What are you doing now?"

"Just ready to go to the store to buy some mais." (This is the German word for corn, and is pronounced with a long "I"—(mize).

"What are you doing with them?"

"Cook and eat. That is our evening meal today."

"Is Jack there?"

"He is outside mowing the grass."

"Get me Jack on the phone now." she said.

I took my purse, the car keys, went to Jack, gave him the message and took off to the store.

In the vegetable department I looked all over for mais.

A young man came to ask me if he could help. I said, "Yes. I am looking for mais." He looked at me as if I was from another world.

He then asked, "What are you doing with them?"

"Cook and eat!"

That young man got so white in his face, said, "Just a minute," and took off.

Shortly after, a gentleman came and said, "I would like to help you. What can I do for you?" he asked.

"I would love to have some mais, even four are OK. It is for our meal tonight."

The man said, "We really do not have mais, but off and on we might get them."

I did not understand what he meant, but it did not sound right to me. I was only about four months in America.

The man went from vegetable to vegetable saying, "Nothing here. Nothing here."

Then I felt he must think I am running from a psychiatric ward. All I could think, "Please, Lord. I need help again."

That minute I saw mais, not in the husk, as I was looking for, but cleaned and in a package. *I believe that was the first time I ever saw mais in a package. I said, loud out, "There are mais!"

He looked at me, probably thinking "that lady really needs help!" I went to him, took my mais and thanked him. He did not say anything, he just looked at me. I walked away to the checkout. The people all around the checkout must have heard the story from the young man. They never were that friendly to me, even gave me a nice "thank you and come back again, Mrs. Larsen."

I told my husband, he was laughing. I said, "I am not going to that store anymore for a long time, and I do not feel like laughing, either."

He said, "I am so very proud of you for not giving up, for not letting your unhappy feelings take control. It would have been so easy to say thank you, turn around, and go home. You chose the only good way to handle your little trouble."

Three weeks later I went back to the store to do my shopping. I was greeted as never before with "Hi, Mrs. Larsen!"

Christmas in America seemed more than an ocean away from Germany, but it was still a wonderful holiday, full of fun. My husband and I always went to the Christmas-tree farm to find a fresh, large tree. Home again, he set the tree in a stand and a day later into our home. My husband put the lights on, I decorated the tree. The tree and I took a lot of praises.

When the tree was ready and all cleaned up, I brought the gifts I bought for my husband to put under the tree. So did my husband.

On Christmas Eve, my husband and I worked together on the meal and setting the table. He was in charge of finding recipes for a meal we had never had before, checked if we had all the spices we needed. If not, he went shopping. We cooked together. He was the man on the stove, watching it cook and tasting. My job was standing across the stove on the counter preparing everything and having it ready for when he needed it,. After every taste, he said, "Perfect!"

We often invited elderly people to spend Christmas Eve with us. The names were given to us by the local Hospital Ladies who called every morning on the elderly. The evening brought lots of joyful talks and singing. Those old kids made us very happy. My husband made always two trips picking six to eight people up. Sometimes all of us went to the candlelight service at church and our guests thanked us with tears running down their cheeks.

I could hardly wait to open my gifts. Among other gifts he could use, I bought Jack a pair of beautiful dress-socks. He loved the socks. He laid them back in the box and I thought, "They are a little expensive for one Christmas." Why was I thinking that? We still had to be very careful with spending money.

When the time came to put all the gifts away, I also kept his socks in the box. A year later I wrapped them again. He admired his socks. The third year, my husband opened the box, smilingly looked at me and said, "Are these the socks you gave to me two years ago?"

"Yes," I said.

He started laughing and said, "You always find something funny." Then he said,
I wonder what will be next!" Well, I will think of something.

Now, my big and heavy box! I pulled a white carrier out, it looked fancy, had a zipper. A big thirteen pound ball with three holes was in there, also, a pair of white shoes which fit perfectly. I looked at that ball a little too long, I believe, when my husband asked, "You like 'em?"

"O, yes," I said, and wondered what I am going to do with that thing. The box said "BOWLING". After a while my husband said, "After I am a little ahead with my work, we will bowl together."

The next day, my husband took Christmas gifts to some kids. I took my ball, rolled them a little in the living room. I thought it was going to hit my beautiful chair. I went after the ball and almost broke my neck! I put that thing back in the carrier and into the trunk in my car.

Some weeks later, I drove along a big main street, when I saw a large sign. "BOWLING!" I thought, "I am going to see if my ball belongs there. I was hardly inside when a lady came running, asking me if I was a bowler.

"Yes," I said. She asked if I would bowl with their team. "Yes, gladly!"

Those rolling balls looked very beautiful to me. I watched what the other women did. I put my shoes on, the ball where it belonged and waited for my turn.

I was the last bowler. I took my little towel. It said, "Happy bowling!" I wiped my ball just like everybody did and walked where I thought I should be. In the other lane, which did not belong to us, stood a girl with her ball in her hands, probably ready to deliver. Yes, I was ready. I did not know I had to wait. I threw my ball. It was fast, crossed into the other girl's lane and threw nine pins down. I really felt too bad for that lady. She looked at her ball in her hands, but the pins went down. Returning to my seat, the girls told me what I can and cannot do, but they wanted to help me. I was lucky we were very good to each other. It took them a long time to let me forget that little excitement. Beautiful, wonderful memories. I became a good bowler. My husband put long boards up in the garage for my trophies.

I know God was always the light on our family's path throughout our lives. It is that one light that has given me the courage to tell my story.

I tell my story because I do not want anybody, not you, your children or grandchildren, to ever go through times like my family and me.

Many prayers and a strong push from God helped me find the courage to talk about our lives. I tell my story so everyone will understand the need for peace.

I am writing my story. I never thought I would do that. Then it came to mind that I have to educate my heart and mind, the key to a better life, love, compassion, and peace. I have seen the good and the bad that life has to offer. It all started in my childhood. But even the bad taught me good lessons for a good life.

Life has fallen into place. We had so much love and respect for life and for each other, and started our days with a thankful heart. I live in peace and contentment.

When my husband, age 75, died, my little world fell in pieces. Unhappiness and loneliness walked with me day and night. My brothers and sisters live in Germany. My friends were there for me. Our senior minister from my church made visits for a long time and helped me to make that little light shine again. I forgot how beautiful life can be, and that I am not alone. I am very thankful to my minister and friends

My husband and I saved the letters we wrote to each other for twenty years, and promised each other that, when we were old, sitting on our porch in our rocking chairs, we would read our love letters to each other. That would bring back loving memories. It did not happen. My best friend, my wonderful life partner who gave me a good life and his unconditional love, died. He walked out of my life as quietly as he came in. I will always be thankful and remember the wonderful years we had together.

Seven years later, and there is still sadness in my heart. I decided that I had to give peace to my Jack and I want my life back, too. I want to be happy again.

I went to the cemetery to my husband's graveside. I told him that he will always have my love and I asked him to let me go, let me go and let me live my life that was given back to me. Let me be happy again.

I went home, even the rainy day brought sunshine into the home and into my heart. I will keep the love I have for my husband in my heart.

The home we made together was hard to give up. Lovely memories were planted in each room. Just about fourteen days before my husband died, he sat in his chair, looked around and said, "I love this home so much." It made me very happy, and I was pleased.

I kept the house for seven more years, took care of the house and the outside. I loved the work, but finally found that I got a little older, too, and it would be better to give up.

The retirement community came just in time to offer me a lovely home. The idea to buy my home and have lifetime care was what I loved. I have a wonderful home, good neighbors, lovely friends, peace, happiness, and a large retirement community and these are the years I can enjoy life without worry. Comes snow or rain, my car and I are safe. Transportation is offered. Now I enjoy activities the retirement community offers in-or-out of the country plus daily nutrition. A medical center is staffed with nurses who will be with you whenever in need.

After my husband died, my little world fell apart, so I adjusted to the lonely days. I did not believe there was another little world waiting for me. Now I can relax and enjoy a "Lifecare" retirement.

And with this poem I will end my story. God bless you.

Rocking Chairs
At certain times of the day,
When light shines through the window
At just the right angle,
I think of him once again.
I remember the dream I had
Of him and I sitting side by side
In our rocking chairs
Rereading old love letters.
He was my life partner
Dreams came true with him.

The love in those letters lived on.
He brought me into his world
And I loved being there.
My life partner walked out of my life
As quietly as he came in.
One rocking chair will stay empty.
My heart will stay so full.
So speak your love.
Speak it again.
Speak it still once again.

Hildegard C. Larsen

Made in the USA
Lexington, KY
12 November 2014